Second Best Jew

Who was the Apostle Paul?

Acts Unpacked

Dr A. T. Bradford MBBS DRCOG MRCGP

Templehouse Publishing ISBN 9781913495053

This book largely draws (unless otherwise indicated) upon the NASB Scripture quotations taken from the New American Standard Bible®, Copyright © 1960, 1962, 1963, 1968, 1971, 1972, 1973, 1975, 1977, 1995 by The Lockman Foundation. Used by permission.

Copyright © 2021-01-024 Dr A .T. Bradford

Published by Templehouse Publishing, London, England.

For other titles by this author please see our website :

www.templehouse-publishing.com

Second Best Jew

Who was the Apostle Paul?

Acts Unpacked

Introduction

If Jesus of Nazareth is globally recognised as the Jew making the greatest ever impact on human history, who would be identified as making the second greatest impact? Surely the Apostle Paul.

A Roman (Turkish) Jewish scholar, a teenage student immigrant to the Jerusalem Temple based school of the great Rabbi Gamaliel, Paul is the writer of over half of the Christian New Testament. No one else comes close in the socio-cultural impact of St Paul on the western world.

Add in the two non-Jewish authored New Testament books of Luke and Acts (written for Paul's trial), the Letter to the Hebrews (written by Paul's disciple Barnabas) and the New Testament influence of Paul becomes almost total. Only three of the four gospels and the writings of Jesus' disciples John and Peter, plus Jesus' half-brothers Jude and James remain.

But just who was Paul? And which Roman family was he from?

To correctly understand the Book of Acts as a letter it is vital to know the identity of both its author (in this case, Luke) and also its recipient (in this case, Theophilus). As well as having an accurate grasp of the letter's historical context and relevant socio-cultural background, it is also essential to understand who the letter's central character was, in this case a Jew with the Hebrew name of Sh'aul (Saul) of Tarsus, (better known today by his Roman name of Paul).

Following on from his first letter to Theophilus, outlining the origins of Jewish messianic faith, the Book of Acts completes Luke's account of the Apostle Paul's legal chronology, ending with Paul under guard in Rome awaiting trial before Caesar for his faith and preaching about Jesus of Nazareth's death and bodily resurrection. The saga would eventually finish with Theophilus succeeding in securing Paul's acquittal and release from Roman imprisonment. That meant that Paul was able to continue his missionary journeys, plant more churches and write the pastoral letters that now comprise the majority of the New Testament.

As a Jewish follower of Messiah, I often wonder why so many Gentile Christians understand Acts to be primarily an immediate history of the life of the early Church. Why then does it end on such a low note? A Roman imprisonment is hardly a ringing endorsement of the victory in Jesus that Paul, the great 'Apostle to the Gentiles', was proclaiming.

Quite simply, Acts was written to supply the eye witness evidence required by Roman jurisprudence for Paul's legal defense from the capital charges of sedition brought against him by the same Jerusalem Temple rulers responsible for Jesus' crucifixion.

While Dr Luke was undoubtedly a first rate historian, he lacked the personal eye witness knowledge of the early Messianic happenings necessary to explain, firsthand, the circumstances surrounding the incarnation, crucifixion and widely reported bodily resurrection appearances of Jesus of Nazareth.

In writing his gospel Luke therefore had to turn to the only surviving person who could tick all of the necessary eye witness boxes - Mary, Jesus' mother. Luke would have had to visit the oldest surviving eye witness to the Gospel narrative, Mary, Jesus' mother. By then Mary was residing with her nephew (John the Evangelist) in the safety of the Greek-Roman city Ephesus (near modern day Izmir in southern Turkey).

That done, Luke turned his attention to the next question that Paul's defense lawyer Theophilus needed an answer to, just how had a good Jewish Temple scholar like Saul got himself into such an awful predicament with his own people? One of that resulted in his being on trial for the potentially capital offence of sedition?

The accusation of subverting Roman authority made by the ruling Judean priests was what ultimately had forced Pontius Pilate's hand in having Jesus executed.

The legal evidence forms the basis of the Book of Acts, where we see Dr Luke first appearing in Troas in around 55 AD (in chapter 16). The introduction of the article 'we' marks the personal arrival of Luke as the narrator.

What follows here is a verse by verse analysis of the original Greek text, written from a particularly Jewish understanding of Paul and the personal (also Jewish) persecutory circumstances that put him on a ship bound for Rome and a legal hearing before Caesar's court following two years of house arrest there.

The main player is of course Sh'aul/Paul, the foremost Jewish legal scholar of his generation and a graduate (Acts 22:3) from the school of the legendary Rabbi Gamaliel, held in Bet Midrash in the Temple in Jerusalem, where Dr Luke (Luke 2:43-52) recorded the twelve year old Jesus having so amazed the Jewish senior teachers several years earlier.

Better known to us by his Roman name Paul, this dual citizen of Rome and Israel was both well off materially and well connected socially in both camps. As shall be shown, and perhaps less well known, he was at least an associate member of the Jews' ruling council, one of the 23 Pharisees who made up the legal scholarship division of the Temple based Sanhedrin. As such he frequently acted legally on behalf of the ruling Jews and priests.

Given that Jesus had taught daily in the Temple, Saul, a slightly younger contemporary, had been extensively exposed to Jesus' extraordinary teaching ministry, enough to feel the extreme pain of personal betrayal at Jesus' apparent breaches of the Jews' prevailing blasphemy laws and so to dedicate himself to eradicating all traces of Jesus' spiritual legacy.

Until his journey to Damascus…

And the rest is history.

Acts Chapter One

1:1-2 'The first account I composed, Theophilus, about all that Jesus began to do and teach until the day when he was taken up to heaven, after he had by the Holy Spirit given orders to the apostles whom he had chosen.'

'Account' here is *'logon'*, often translated as 'treatise', a legal document. Luke is referring to his first collection of manuscripts previously sent to Theophilus and known today as Luke's Gospel. Cross-referencing over to Luke chapter 1, we can note the profuse legalese used by Dr Luke in his prologue.

It is therefore reasonable to conclude that Luke was writing to a lawyer and providing eye-witness testimony. Who else was alive in the 60s AD and a witness of the nativity other than Jesus' mother Mary?

This point, taken together with Luke's use of *'kratistos'* ('most excellent'), confirms Theophilus' identity as a senior lawyer (or judge), commonly drawn from the highly educated equestrian section of Roman society. Luke's use of *'kratistos'* in reference to two Roman ruler-judges Felix and Festus (Acts 25 and 26), further confirms this view, as does the fact that Acts closes with Paul under arrest and awaiting his trial in Rome on the potentially capital charge of sedition. Paul needed a good lawyer and Luke, the 'beloved physician' (Colossians 4:14), provided and instructed one.

Luke's Gospel and Acts may therefore be seen as forming the formal legal chronology of Paul's defense against the Jews' accusations.

Having already outlined the origins of the newly emerged Messianic faith, Luke is now ready to relate to Theophilus exactly how Paul, a Jewish religious scholar from a wealthy and reputable Roman family could have become embroiled in such difficulties with his fellow Jews in both Asia and Judea. These difficulties extended to their pressing formal charges with the ruling Roman hierarchy in the Roman's local centre of government (Caesarea Philippi) after failing in multiple attempts to murder Paul because of his newfound faith in Jesus as the promised Messiah.

Jesus is described by Dr Luke as the Jewish Messiah (Christ), the divine and anointed authority figure who is still 'doing and teaching' today. 'Given orders' (verse 2) is *'enteilamenos'*, a Roman military term also meaning 'commanded', from the Greek *'entelomai'* - 'military orders emphasizing reaching an end-objective.'

Throughout Acts we will see Luke (a Roman) deliberately using very Roman-friendly language and describing particularly Roman-friendly events in Paul's life with a view to bolstering Paul's likelihood of judicial acquittal at his forthcoming trial. Theophilus is now introduced to the bac k story concerning how Paul gained his role as an apostle.

'Apostles' (verse 2) is *'apostolois'* - one sent out on a mission.

Jesus was speaking 'by the Spirit'. It is necessary to tune in to that same Holy Spirit to be able to hear him speaking directly today. 'Taken up into heaven' refers to Jesus' ascension, already described by Luke in chapter 24 of his gospel.

Jesus' apostles had all been 'chosen' - *'exelexato'* – an active choice of the 12 apostles, including Judas Iscariot. His disciples represented a broad range of religious Jews, already described by Luke in his first (gospel) treatise.

Jesus had chosen his twelve apostles, after a night of prayerful communion with his heavenly Father. Judas Iscariot was chosen, for purposes then foreknown only by God. Judas was a complex individual and I unpack the reasons for his apostolic selection in my commentary on John's Gospel, 'Joseph in John, Judas and Jewish Jokes.' Suffice to say here that he played an essential and necessary role in God's eternal plan of salvation.

1:3: 'These he also presented himself to alive after his suffering, by many convincing proofs, appearing to them over *a* period *of* forty days and speaking of the things concerning the kingdom of God.'

By mentioning 'convincing proofs', Luke is again emphasizing to Theophilus the validity and legally strong nature of his treatise. The Greek term used here is '*tekmēriois*',, meaning 'evidential material' and likely to carry weight in the pending Roman legal proceedings.

Jesus' multiple post-resurrection appearances, combined with a continuation of the miraculous demonstrations of divine power that had so characterised his ministry were all sufficiently attested to as to be relied upon before a Roman Court.

'Forty days' carries a particular Jewish significance, evoking the length of Jesus' fast in the desert at the commencement of his ministry and, additionally, the forty days spent by Moses receiving the Torah on Mount Sinai.

1:4-5: 'Gathering them together, he commanded them not to leave Jerusalem, but to wait for what the Father had promised, "Which," he said, "you heard of from me; for John baptized with water, but you will be baptized with the Holy Spirit not many days from now."'

Jesus reminds the group of believers of what they had been taught concerning the coming of the Holy Spirit. Jesus' cousin John the Baptist had told the Jews gathering by the River Jordan for his water baptism that 'among them was one who would baptize with the Holy Spirit'., and Jesus had spent much of his final days before the crucifixion teaching them of the ministry of the '*paraklete*', the One 'who comes alongside to help'. Soon this third member of the Godhead would be in them, filling and empowering them in living for God.

1:6 'So when they had come together, they were asking him, saying, "Lord, is it at this time you are restoring the kingdom to Israel?"

Restoring' is *'apokathistémi'*, meaning to 're-establish to its original condition'. In Israel's case this meant to its place as 'top nation', as in the era of King David. While very understandable from a nationalistic and even a spiritual perspective, this sentiment was unlikely to have been well received in a Roman court.

Luke therefore emphasizes Jesus' politically neutral response, namely that such matters are entirely at Father God's disposal. Jesus had spoken often and extensively about the judgment coming upon the spiritually obese and complacently corrupt nation that Israel had become under the rule of its religious elite, both corrupt priests and legalistic Pharisees.

1:7 'He said to them, "It is not for you to know times or epochs which the Father has fixed by His own authority.'

Jesus' deflection of his disciples' religious nationalism can be seen as not being in any way critical of the God ordained prevailing rule of Rome. His all seeing heavenly Father had fixed a times for nations to rise and fall, this being information that we are not always privy to.

1:8 "But you will receive power when the Holy Spirit has come upon you; ad you shall be my witnesses both in Jerusalem, and in all Judea and Samaria, and even to the remotest part of the earth."'

Jesus' disciples had no knowledge of God's timetable but instead had *'dynamin'* – 'miraculous power', which is not a bad alternative. This power would enable them to be *'martyres'* –' eye-witnesses' - another Roman legal term, derived from *'martus'* - 'witness'. Their witness would eventually lead all except John to violent deaths.

1:9 'And after he had said these things, he was lifted up while they were looking on, and a cloud received him out of their sight.'

Luke now returns to his description of Jesus' ascension described in Luke 24:31. 'Taken up' is *'epērthē'* - a nautical term used in describing hoisting a foresail, as, for example, in Acts 27:40.

1:10-11 'And as they were gazing intently into the sky while He was going, behold, two men in white clothing stood beside them. They also said, "Men of Galilee, why do you stand looking into the sky? This Jesus, who has been taken up from you into heaven, will come in just the same way as you have watched him go into heaven."'

Angels now make an appearance. Luke's intended Roman audience (unlike the Jewish Sadducees and the priesthood,) acknowledged angels' existence as a kind of heavenly postmen without actually offering them worship. The information that these two messengers deliver is effectively "Jesus will be coming back in the same way he went, so best not stand there gaping but instead do something useful."

1:10 'Then they returned to Jerusalem from the mount called Olivet, which is near Jerusalem, a Sabbath day's journey away'.

The Mount of Olives was the hill adjacent to Temple Mount and the scene of their last Judean adventure with Jesus, which had resulted in Jesus' arrest in the garden of Gethsemane.

It lay just outside the direct jurisdiction of the ruling Sanhedrin and as such was relatively safe for the apostles, men who could reasonably expect to be next on the ruling Jews' list of men deemed subversive enough to warrant taking drastic measures against.

1:13 'When they had entered the city, they went up to the upper room where they were staying; that is, Peter and John and James and Andrew, Philip and Thomas, Bartholomew and Matthew, James the son of Alphaeus, and Simon the Zealot, and Judas the son of James.

Jesus had celebrated his final Passover meal with his disciples in the large first floor guest room of the Jerusalem guest house probably owned by the Essenes, a largely celibate Jewish religious movement best known nowadays for its preservation of the Dead Sea scrolls.

The eleven Apostles, following the suicide of Judas Iscariot, encompassed men from across the spectrum of first century Jewish religious life, these men had been prayerfully selected by Jesus to be trained in readiness for eventually replacing him.

These eyewitnesses were not actually witnessing. Rather, they were praying, and with women too. This culturally very unusual behaviour for first century Judean religious Jews doubtless followed the pattern established by Jesus himself, soon to be carried forward by his latest apostle in waiting, Saul of Tarsus.

1:14 'These all with one mind were continually devoting themselves to prayer, along with the women, and Mary the mother of Jesus, and with his brothers.'

Not only was the inner circle of women headed by Jesus' mother Mary present but also her naturally conceived sons - James, Joses/Joseph), Simeon and Judas/Jude (Mark 6:3).

'With one mind' is '*homothymadon*', from '*homou*' and '*thumos* - 'unanimously' and 'with one accord', as in John 17- 'they may all be one'. This attitude is vital to effectual collective prayer.

1:15 'At this time Peter stood up in the midst of the brethren (a gathering of about one hundred and twenty persons was there together)'

Peter, James and John jointly led the early church until the eventual delegation of this role to Jesus' now believing eldest half-brother James, a man of great piety and in good standing with the Sanhedrin.

1:16 'and said, "Brethren, the Scripture had to be fulfilled, which the Holy Spirit foretold by the mouth of David concerning Judas, who became a guide to those who arrested Jesus.'"

Judas Iscariot, acting in accordance with the absolute will of God, had delivered Jesus up to the Sanhedrin, with Jesus' prior knowledge and cooperation. His history with the Iscarri, who were well recorded assassins of religious leaders felt to be falling short of their radical Jewish liberationists' aspirations meant that he was ideally suited to this necessarily murderous role.

Iscarri were the extreme wing of the Zealots movement, these being radical Jews who made up a significant proportion of Jewish first century society. Simon the Zealot, like Judas, was one of the twelve men selected by Jesus to the role of Apostle.

1:17 "'For he was counted among us and received his share in this ministry."

Judas had been personally selected to be one of the twelve men to whom Jesus would deliver the maximum personally formative teaching. Was that all wasted in Judas' case? Judas' seat of honour at the Last Supper (John 13:26), and Jesus' addressing him as 'friend' in the garden of Gethsemane (Matthew 26:50) suggest that it was not.

1:18-19 '(Now this man acquired a field with the price of his wickedness, and falling headlong, he burst open in the middle and all his intestines gushed out. And it became known to all who were living in Jerusalem; so that in their own language that field was called Hakeldama, that is, Field of Blood.)'

'Wickedness' is *'akidia'*, which Vine's Dictionary defines as 'unrighteous according to the standard known to be right by conscience'. Judas' conscience drove him to commit suicide. There is no Scriptural support for the notion of him being consigned to hell.

Matthew 27:3-10 records: 'Then when Judas, who had betrayed him, saw that he had been condemned, he felt remorse and returned the thirty pieces of silver to the Chief Priests and elders, saying, 'I have sinned by betraying innocent blood.' But they said, 'What is that to us? See to that yourself!' And he threw the pieces of silver into the Temple sanctuary and departed; and he went away and hanged himself. The Chief Priests took the pieces of silver and said, 'It is not lawful to put them into the Temple treasury, since it is the price of blood.' And they conferred, together and with the money bought the Potter's Field as a burial place for strangers. For this reason that field has been called the Field of Blood to this day. Then that which was spoken through Jeremiah the prophet was fulfilled: 'And they took the thirty pieces of silver, the price of the one whose price had been set by the sons of Israel, and they gave them for the Potter's Field, as the Lord directed me.'

There was therefore a double fulfillment of this prophesy - the money was thrown to God (the Heavenly Potter) in the house of God - the Temple, and it was then used to purchase 'the Potter's Field'.

1:20 "'For it is written in the book of Psalms, 'Let his homestead be left desolate, and let no one dwell in it'; and, 'Let another man take his place of office.'

Peter cites two Psalms, Psalm 69:25, 'May their camp be desolate; may none dwell in their tents' and Psalm 109:8, 'Let his days be few; let another take his office', in support of replacing Judas. Peter and Luke give no indication at all of this action having been prompted by God.

1:21-22 "'Therefore it is necessary that of the men who have accompanied us all the time that the Lord Jesus went in and out among us - beginning with the baptism of John until the day that he was taken up from us - one of these must become a witness with us of his resurrection.'"

Peter evidently felt the need to replace Judas, perhaps to maintain the numeric parallel with that selected by Jesus, reflecting the number of the tribes of Israel. He could not in his wildest dreams have imagined that God already had a plan to bring into the apostolic ranks Rabbi Gamaliel's current foremost disciple.

As a formidable Temple scholar, a Bet Midrash based contemporary and now a ferocious enemy of Jesus' spiritual legacy, Saul of Tarsus was an extremely unlikely choice of replacement. But exactly typical of a choice God would make, and for excellent reasons.

1:23-26 'So they put forward two men, Joseph called Barsabbas (who was also called Justus), and Matthias. And they prayed and said, "You, Lord, who know the hearts of all men, show which one of these two you have chosen to occupy this ministry and apostleship from which Judas turned aside to go to his own place." And they drew lots for them, and the lot fell to Matthias; and he was added to the eleven apostles.'

'Drawing lots was an Old Covenant practice, described in 1 Chronicles 24:5, that was soon to become a thing of the past with the coming of the Counselor, the promised Holy Spirit, who would take what was Jesus' and reveal it to his disciples (John 16:15).

Matthias, good man though he undoubtedly was, is never heard of again.

Saul, on the other hand...

Chapter Two

Acts 2:1 'When the day of Pentecost had come, they were all together in one place.'

Jesus' promise of Acts 1:8 is now about to be gloriously fulfilled. Pentecost, in addition to being a harvest celebration and a compulsory feast, also commemorated the giving of the Law to Moses on Mount Sinai by the pre-incarnate Son of God, written with his own finger on tablets of stone (Exodus 19-24).

Under Jesus' New Covenant of grace this legal framework would later translate into the law of God being written on 'tablets of human hearts' (Jeremiah 31:33, 2 Corinthians 3:3), by the Holy Spirit who was about to be outpoured.

2:2. 'And suddenly there came from heaven a noise like a violent rushing wind, and it filled the whole house where they were sitting.'

Without warning, a hurricane apparently struck the house. The only conceivable human reaction from the praying disciples to this unprecedented phenomenon is sudden and severe shock.

2:3 'And there appeared to them tongues as of fire distributing themselves, and they rested on each one of them.'

And now these praying Jews appear to spontaneously combust! Shock turns into panic as each sees flames on the rest. There being no previous example in Israel's history of such unexpected events occurring, so the praying apostles would have been taken completely by surprise.

2:4 'And they were all filled with the Holy Spirit and began to speak with other tongues, as the Spirit was giving them utterance.'

The disciples, hit by a hurricane and now actually set on fire, start to jabber in unknown languages. Their minds simply cannot compute either the sudden hurricane or the flames and, in a state of great shock, probably bordering on panic, they rush from the building.

Outside they find that others have gathered, pilgrim Jews who have also heard the sudden noise of the 'violent wind', and naturally come to investigate.

2:5 'Now there were Jews living in Jerusalem, devout men from every nation under heaven. And when this sound occurred, the crowd came together, and were bewildered because each one of them was hearing them speak in his own language.'

Pentecost was one of the three feasts of Israel at which attendance was compulsory for all adult Jewish males residing within the Holy Land. The mixed race Jewish festival crowd had heard the noise of the hurricane and now they hear something even more intriguing.

2:6-11 'They were amazed and astonished, saying, "Why, are not all these who are speaking Galileans? And how is it that we each hear them in our own language to which we were born? Parthians and Medes and Elamites, and residents of Mesopotamia, Judea and Cappadocia, Pontus and Asia, Phrygia and Pamphylia, Egypt and the districts of Libya around Cyrene, and visitors from Rome, both Jews and proselytes, Cretans and Arabs - we hear them in our own tongues speaking of the mighty deeds of God."'

The apostles, being largely from Israel's northern region of Galilee, were easily distinguishable from the residents of Jerusalem by their strong Aramaic dialect, as Matthew 26:73 makes clear.

The pilgrim crowd, being similarly 'foreign', listened in amazement to these Galilean apostles' superb and supernatural mastery of their many and varied dialects and languages.

The Parthians had come from the immediate east, as far as the Persian Gulf (modern day Iraq). Babylon was its capital city.

Media was the region slightly further north and east (modern day Iran), whereas Elam was the region north of the Persian Gulf between Iran and Iraq.

Mesopotamia was the region of the Tigris and Euphrates to the north and west, as far as the Taurus. Under the

Greek Seleucid rule, modern Syria was regarded as part of its kingdom.

Cappadocia is now modern day central Turkey and Pontus was a Persian state situated around the Black Sea.

Asia refers to the region on the eastern shore of the Aegean Sea, which was occupied by the Romans in 190BC and Phrygia lay on the western end of the high Anatolian plateau between the Black Sea and the Mediterranean Sea.

Pamphylia was the region of the southern Anatolian peninsula, and Cyrene was the capital city of a Greek colony in modern day Libya, some of whom may well have originated in the Mediterranean island of Crete.

All in all it was a very international group of pilgrim Jews, selected by God to carry the good news of this divine intervention home with them after their religious festival was over.

The 'mighty deeds of God', of which the Apostles spoke, under the direct influence of the Holy Spirit, would certainly have included Jesus' birth, life, death and resurrection. Hence the gospel message was being powerfully proclaimed.

2:12-13 'And they all continued in amazement and great perplexity, saying to one another, "What does this mean?" But others were mocking and saying, "They are full of sweet wine."'

Some listen but some mock, accusing the apostles of inebriation.

2:14 'But Peter, taking his stand with the eleven, raised his voice and declared to them: "Men of Judea, and all you who live in Jerusalem, let this be known to you and give heed to my words."'

Peter, as one of the inner circle of the three closest disciples of Jesus, represents the rest of the apostles in stating that alcohol has played no part in the proceedings, but that an important prophetic fulfillment is taking place.

2:15-21 '"For these men are not drunk, as you suppose, for it is only the third hour of the day; but this is what was spoken of through the prophet Joel: "It will come about after this that I will pour out my Spirit on all mankind, and your sons and daughters will prophesy, your old men will dream dreams, your young men will see visions. Even on the male and female servants I will pour out my Spirit in those days. I will display wonders in the sky and on the earth, blood, fire and columns of smoke. The sun will be turned into darkness and the moon into blood before the great and awesome day of the Lord comes. And it will come about that whoever calls on the name of the Lord will be delivered; for on Mount Zion and in Jerusalem there will be those who escape, as the Lord has said, even among the survivors whom the Lord calls."'

Speaking under the anointing influence of the Holy Spirit Peter cites the ninth century BC prophet Joel who had said:

'It will come about after this that I will pour out my Spirit on all mankind; and your sons and daughters will prophesy, your old men will dream dreams, your young men will see visions. Even on the male and female servants I will pour out My Spirit in those days. I will display wonders in the sky and on the earth, blood, fire and columns of smoke. The sun will be turned into darkness and the moon into blood before the great and awesome day of the Lord comes. And it will come about that whoever calls on the name of the Lord will be delivered; for on Mount Zion and in Jerusalem there will be those who escape, as the Lord has said, even among the survivors whom the Lord calls.' (Joel 2:28-32).

The mighty rushing wind was certainly a 'wonder in the sky', and human beings spontaneously set alight in a burning bush manner (Exodus 3:1-17) were not exactly an everyday occurrence either. Peter had been told by Jesus to expect the baptism in the Holy Spirit, and the attendant gift of speaking in a tongue unknown to the speaker was the first recorded instance of the use of what would be experienced in a variety of different contexts within the early church.

2:22-24 "'Men of Israel, listen to these words: Jesus the Nazarene, a man attested to you by God with miracles and wonders and signs which God performed through him in your midst, just as you yourselves know - this man, delivered over by the predetermined plan and foreknowledge of God, you nailed to a cross by the hands of godless men and put him to death. But God raised him up again, putting an end to the agony of death, since it was impossible for him to be held in its power.'"

Jesus' fame as a miracle working Temple Torah teacher was very well established and needed no explanation. His death by recent public crucifixion was similarly well known. His resurrection was less well known, and it is this evidence of power over death that Peter draws the crowd's attention to.

Peter then cites Psalm 16:8-11, supporting the fact that Messiah would taste death but defeat it 'without decay' (through bodily resurrection).

2:25-28: "'For David says of him, 'I saw the Lord always in my presence; for he is at my right hand, so that I will not be shaken. Therefore my heart was glad and my tongue exulted; moreover my flesh also will live in hope; because you will not abandon my soul to hades, nor allow your Holy One to undergo decay. You have made known to me the ways of life; you will make me full of gladness with your presence.'"

Peter then follows this up by again proclaiming Jesus' resurrection, in comparison with the greatest but all too mortal King David.

2:29-33 "'Brethren, I may confidently say to you regarding the patriarch David that he both died and was buried, and his tomb is with us to this day. And so, because he was a prophet and knew that God had sworn to him with an oath to seat one of his descendants on his throne he looked ahead and spoke of the resurrection of the Christ, that he was neither abandoned to Hades, nor did his flesh suffer decay. This Jesus God raised up again, to which we are all witnesses. Therefore having been exalted to the right hand of God, and having received from the Father the promise of the Holy Spirit, He has poured forth this, which you both see and hear.'"

Hades was the Greek equivalent term for Sheol (also meaning 'grave'), the Hebrew name for the place of the souls of the dead prior to judgment.

It is a place that Jesus had often spoken of and the place of human souls awaiting judgment after dying devoid of saving faith was therefore something that Peter would have been very familiar with. He later wrote:

'For Christ also died for sins once for all, the just for the unjust, so that he might bring us to God, having been put to death in the flesh, but made alive in the spirit; in which also he went and made proclamation to the spirits now in prison.' (1 Peter 3:18-19.)

Jesus had had proclamation work to do after dying and before his bodily resurrection and having done it he was 'exalted' to God the Father's right hand - *'hypsōtheis'*, from *'hupsos'*, meaning 'to elevate'. Back in heaven,

Jesus then poured out his promised Holy Spirit (John 14:16-18) on his waiting infant church.

2:34-36 "'For it was not David who ascended into heaven, but he himself says, 'The Lord said to my Lord, "Sit at my right hand until I make your enemies a footstool for your feet."' Therefore let all the house of Israel know for certain that God has made him both Lord and Christ - this Jesus whom you crucified.'"

Peter recalls and quotes Jesus' own teaching (Matthew 22:42-46) on Psalm 16, and contrasts the all too human David with Jesus the promised Messiah. Peter, speaking under the Spirit's inspiration, declares the guilty role that his audience had played in Jesus' death, either directly through their presence in the crowds before Pilate or indirectly through their personal sin.

2:37-39 'Now when they heard this, they were pierced to the heart, and said to Peter and the rest of the apostles, "Brethren, what shall we do?" Peter said to them, "Repent, and each of you be baptized in the name of Jesus Christ for the forgiveness of your sins; and you will receive the gift of the Holy Spirit. "For the promise is for you and your children and for all who are far off, as many as the Lord our God will call to himself."'

'Piercing to the heart' is something that only the all-seeing Spirit of God is able to accomplish, however good the human orator. Peter then summarizes the process of spiritual conversion. The change of mind/thinking of repentance and being baptized (with an attitude of faith) are things that are the individual believers' responsibility to do, while forgiveness and the receiving of the Holy Spirit are the gracious direct gifts of God.

In addition to Joel, the promise of the Holy Spirit had also been given by Isaiah (44:3 and 59:21) hence have been a familiar, though previously never experienced, concept to Peter's religious pilgrim audience

2:40-42 'And with many other words he solemnly testified and kept on exhorting them, saying, "Be saved from this perverse generation!" So then, those who had received his word were baptized; and that day there were added about three thousand souls. They were continually devoting themselves to the apostles' teaching and to fellowship, to the breaking of bread and to prayer.'

The 'perverse' generation' is, in the Greek, *'skolias'*, meaning 'twisted' or 'crooked'. It was this generation against which Jesus had uttered the following prophetic lament:

"Jerusalem, Jerusalem, who kills the prophets and stones those who are sent to her! How often I wanted to gather your children together, the way a hen gathers her chicks under her wings, and you were unwilling. "Behold, your house is being left to you desolate! "For I say to you, from now on you will not see me until you say, 'Blessed is he who comes in the name of the Lord!'" (Matthew 23:37-39).

And before that, Jesus had addressed the root of the problem, which was their underlying evil nature
.

Matthew 12:43-45 records:

"'Now when an unclean spirit goes out of a man, it passes through waterless places seeking rest, and does not find it. Then it says, 'I will return to my house from which I came'; and when it comes, it finds it unoccupied, swept, and put in order. Then it goes and takes along with it seven other spirits more wicked than itself, and they go in and live there; and the last state of that man becomes worse than the first. That is the way it will also be with this evil generation."

'Evil' here is *'poneros',* meaning 'toilsome' or, as Strong's dictionary puts it 'pressed and harassed by labours'.

Jesus was addressing the Jewish Scribes and Pharisees, the men responsible for multiplying religious legalism and then insisting that their pronouncements be adhered to as though from God himself. Their refusal to accept Jesus' identity as God incarnate and the grace offered by him brought upon their generation of Jewish scholarship a completion of the disciplines outlined in Deuteronomy 28:16-68 as consequences of unfaithfulness.

Jesus was prophetically foreseeing the outpouring of judgment upon that generation within Israel, culminating in the destruction of the Temple in AD 70.

The prophet Daniel (9:27) had centuries earlier predicted the abomination that Antiochus Epiphanes, the king of Syria, would introduce by sacrificing a pig on the Temple altar, a sacrilegious act which provoked the Maccabean revolt of 166-162 BC.

A similar abomination would occur again in 70 AD when, as Josephus ('Wars', 5,6,1) records, 'The Romans, upon the flight of the seditious into the city, and upon the burning of the holy house itself, and of all the buildings round about it, brought their ensigns to the Temple and set them over against its eastern gate; and there did they offer sacrifices to them.'

Jesus also prophesied the flight from Jerusalem that would necessarily occur if his followers were to survive the city's siege and the onslaught of the encircling Roman army.

Eusebius the Bishop of Caesarea (263-339 AD) later recorded the actions of the disciples when they saw the Roman army under the command of Vespasian preparing to besiege the city of Jerusalem:

'The whole body, however, of the church at Jerusalem, having been commanded by a divine revelation, given to men of approved piety there before the war, removed from the city, and dwelt at a certain town beyond the Jordan, called Pella. Here those that believed in Jesus, having removed from Jerusalem, as if holy men had entirely abandoned the royal city itself, and the whole land of Judea; the divine justice, for their crimes against Jesus and his apostles finally overtook them, totally destroying the whole generation of these evildoers form the earth' (Eusebius, 3:5).

Peter's message, combined with the conviction and anointing of the Holy Spirit, resulted in many of his pilgrim audience 'receiving' (*'apodexamenoi'* – 'accepting fully, embracing') with faith and being baptized before engaging with Messiah's teaching as delivered to his disciples.

These thousands of men and women, from a very wide geographic area, would take the gospel in the power of the Spirit back to their respective cities and communities.

They also became engaged in fellowship (*'koinonia'* - 'common partnership/participation'). This community mentality, born out of the grace explosion of Pentecost, is illustrated by the sharing of material goods and possessions described in verses 44 and 45. The 'breaking of bread' referenced as the third outworking of this new grace is mentioned again in verse 46 and illustrates the sharing of food as part of their daily fellowship with one another. This may well have included the 'agape' meals with a focus on sharing the new covenant cup that Jesus had inaugurated at his final Seder meal. The fourth attribute of the infant church was prayer. This is *'proseuché'*, from *'prós'* ('exchange') and *'euxe'* ('wishes'). Prayer is therefore an 'exchange of wishes' with God.

2:43-47 'Everyone kept feeling a sense of awe; and many wonders and signs were taking place through the apostles. And all those who had believed were together and had all things in common; and they began selling their property and possessions and were sharing them with all, as anyone might have need. Day by day continuing with one mind in the temple, and breaking bread from house to house, they were taking their meals together with gladness and sincerity of heart, praising God and having favour with all the people. And the Lord was adding to their number day by day those who were being saved.'

'Awe' is *'phobos'* - 'fear' (of God), an appropriate response to any powerful move of the Spirit where the miraculous has become commonplace. God's grace for the commonality of koinonia even led to the selling and sharing of property, an extraordinary reversal of sinful human nature born out of the fruit of the Spirit, generosity.

The believers lost all fear of the Jewish religious authorities and gravitated to the Temple Courts, thereby continuing the ministry of propagating the Kingdom of God that Jesus' arrest and execution had interrupted. This building of the new spiritual house of the Church was conducted by God himself - the God who had said 'Unless the Lord builds the house, they labour in vain who build it.' (Psalm 127:1)

Chapter 3

3:1-2 'Now Peter and John were going up to the temple at the ninth hour, the hour of prayer. And a man who had been lame from his mother's womb was being carried along, whom they used to set down every day at the gate of the Temple which is called Beautiful, in order to beg alms of those who were entering the Temple.'

The grace filled normalcy of relations with the Jewish religious authorities at that time, was such that Temple attendance at the regular times of Priest-led prayers was still being observed.

The Jewish day was divided into twelve equal parts; the ninth hour was three o'clock in the afternoon. This was the hour of evening prayer. Morning Prayers were offered at nine am. The beggar in question, profiting from the religious duty of worshippers to give alms, was most likely suffering from a congenital vertebral abnormality such as spina bifida, where imperfect fusion of the vertebral bodies in utero results in spinal nerve root pressure and consequential lower limb paralysis. He would have had a regular 'pitch' at the Temple gate and was doubtless passed on many occasions by Jesus without it being God the Father's time for his healing to be performed. Now the day had finally arrived.

3:3-5 'When he saw Peter and John about to go into the temple, he began asking to receive alms. But Peter, along with John, fixed his gaze on him and said, "Look at us!" And he began to give them his attention, expecting to receive something from them.'

The 'fixed gaze' that both apostles turn upon the beggar indicates that something spiritual is likely to be happening, this is no quick glance but rather a moment of divine communication and faith igniting inspiration. There is evidently no faith being displayed by the beggar, rather his expectation is purely financial.

3:6-8 'But Peter said, "I do not possess silver and gold, but what I do have I give to you: In the name of Jesus Christ the Nazarene - walk!" And seizing him by the right hand, he raised him up; and immediately his feet and his ankles were strengthened. With a leap he stood upright and began to walk; and he entered the Temple with them, walking and leaping and praising God.'

Holding the lame man's gaze and attention Peter continues in what the Apostles had certainly extensive personal training from Jesus in, the performance of the miraculous. Peter's legs had learned, through faith, to walk on water. His faith had now enabled him to hear a word from God concerning God's intention to heal the lame man, and so in complete confidence, he grabs the beggar and hauls him to his feet. There is no spoken prayer, no explanation, nothing is done to spiritually prepare the lame man to receive divine healing, nothing at all!

It is simply an unembellished demonstration of the power of Almighty God, who at that very instant transformed the wasted and useless lower limb musculature into normal adult functioning entities. The beggar's reaction to this unexpected turn of events is telling. This was surely a Jewish man known and loved by God long before this eventful day.

His jumping up and down and hurried Temple entrance to join with the rest of Jerusalem's praying community clearly shows a heart open and receptive to a personal knowledge and love of God that pours forth vocal praise.

3:9-10 'And all the people saw him walking and praising God; and they were taking note of him as being the one who used to sit at the Beautiful Gate of the temple to beg alms, and they were filled with wonder and amazement at what had happened to him.'

The residents of Jerusalem were very familiar with the beggar, having daily passed him for many decades. Seeing him now leaping up and down with joy and excitement at what had so unexpectedly happened to him, the Temple crowd is struck with a profound sense of *'thambous'* ('awe/amazed stupefaction') and *'ekstasis'* ('a displacement of the mind/ bewilderment'), from *'existimi'*, meaning 'to throw into wonderment'.

3:11 'While he was clinging to Peter and John, all the people ran together to them at the so-called portico of Solomon, full of amazement.'

Solomon's Porch/Portico was located on the eastern side of the court of the women in the Temple. Josephus Flavius, a Jewish-Roman historian who was present at the destruction of Jerusalem by the Romans under

Vaspasian in 70 A.D., wrote of the wall and of the cloister or porch that Solomon had built east of the Holy Place:
'Now this temple, as I have already said, was built upon a strong hill. At first the plain at the top was hardly sufficient for the holy house and the altar, for the ground about it was very uneven, and like a precipice; but when King Solomon, who was the person that built the temple, had built a wall to it on its east side, there was then added one cloister founded on a bank cast up for it, and on the other parts the holy house stood naked.'

The dimensions of Herod's Temple formed a square - a furlong by a furlong on all four sides. On the east wall was a double cloister or porch, commonly referred to as Solomon's Porch:

Josephus further relates: 'The Temple hill was walled all round, and in compass four furlongs, [the distance of] each angle containing in length a furlong: but within this wall, and on the very top of all, there ran another wall of stone also, having, on the east quarter, a double cloister, of the same length with the wall; in the midst of which was the Temple itself. This cloister looked towards the gates of the temple; and it had been adorned by many kings in former times; and round about the entire temple were fixed the spoils taken from barbarous nations; all these had been dedicated to the temple by Herod, with the addition of those he had taken from the Arabians.'

Josephus ('Antiquities' 15, 11, 3) is clear that Herod refused to let his priest-builders make any changes in the ancient works of the east wall because of the great expense. He allowed the construction of new courts on the north, west and south sides of the Temple but the existing site's east wall remained intact and undisturbed.

The cloister/porch provided space where the still very 'astounded' crowd could congregate around the apostles and the miraculously healed man, who yet to fully come to terms with the sudden turn of events, is holding on tightly (literally 'seized') to the apostles through whom the miracle had occurred.

3:22-16 'But when Peter saw this, he replied to the people, "Men of Israel, why are you amazed at this, or why do you gaze at us, as if by our own power or piety we had made him walk? The God of Abraham, Isaac and Jacob, the God of our fathers, has glorified his servant

Jesus, the one whom you delivered and disowned in the presence of Pilate, when he had decided to release him. But you disowned the Holy and Righteous One and asked for a murderer to be granted to you, but put to death the Prince of life, the one whom God raised from the dead, a fact to which we are witnesses. And on the basis of faith in his name, it is the name of Jesus which has strengthened this man whom you see and know; and the faith which comes through him has given him this perfect health in the presence of you all.'

Again the Holy Spirit gives Peter words that clearly place responsibility for the unjust execution of Jesus on the members of the Jerusalem public, many of whom would have been in the crowd that, encouraged by the priests, called upon a reluctant Pilate to release Barabbas and deliver Jesus to death (Luke 23:18, John 18:40).

Peter presents the fact of the miracle as evidence of God's glorification (*'edoxasen'*) – 'to honour/bestow glory upon' Jesus, whose name and power Peter credits for the miracle.

3:17-21 'And now, brethren, I know that you acted in ignorance, just as your rulers did also. But the things which God announced beforehand by the mouth of all the prophets, that his Christ would suffer, he has thus fulfilled. Therefore repent and return, so that your sins may be wiped away, in order that times of refreshing may come from the presence of the Lord; and that he may send Jesus, the Christ appointed for you, whom heaven must receive until the period of restoration of all things about which God spoke by the mouth of his holy prophets from ancient time.'

The ignorant (and sinful) actions of the people and their leaders were all foreknown by the God who dwells outside the realm of time yet who intervenes in human history through his prophets and now, much more significantly, through his incarnate self, Messiah, the pre-existent second person of the triune Godhead.

If the people repent of their sins (*'metanoēsate'* -'to think differently and in consequence change behaviour') and return (*'epistrepsate'* – from *'strephó'*, 'to return/revert', and *'epi'*, 'upon'), then God will send them more grace in the form of 'times of refreshing', culminating in the second and final coming of Messiah, as prophesied of old.

3:22-26 'Moses said, 'The Lord God will raise up for you a prophet like me from among your brethren; to him you shall give heed to everything he says to you. And it will be that be that every soul that does not heed that prophet shall be utterly destroyed from among the people.' And likewise, all the prophets who have spoken, from Samuel and his successors onward, also announced these days. It is you who are the sons of the prophets and of the covenant which God made with your fathers, saying to Abraham, 'And in your seed all the families of the earth shall be blessed.' For you first, God raised up his Servant and sent him to bless you by turning every one of you from your wicked ways.'"

Moses' prophetic insight into the coming of another (like him) educated Jew was a clear and very well recognized reference to Messiah. Moses had grown up and been educated in all the wisdom of the Egyptians in a hidden capacity within Pharaoh's palace before commencing his redemptive mission. Jesus had grown up and been Torah educated in Bet Midrash in Herod's Temple, but in a hidden capacity as far as his divinity was concerned, prior to publically commencing his redemptive mission. Both had been initially rejected by their own people.

As the direct descendants of Abraham, the Messiah had come to them first, with the blessing of salvation through sins being forgiven.

Chapter 4

4:1-4 'As they were speaking to the people, the priests and the captain of the temple guard and the Sadducees came up to them, being greatly disturbed because they were teaching the people and proclaiming in Jesus the resurrection from the dead. And they laid hands on them and put them in jail until the next day, for it was already evening. But many of those who had heard the message believed; and the number of the men came to be about five thousand.'

Finally, the religious police appear. The Temple Courts were supervised closely by its resident priests, who had a squad of Roman trained priest/soldier-guards at their disposal, led by a Roman trained Captain and supported by the Roman military garrison housed in the adjoining Roman fort of Antonia at the Temple's northeast corner.

The fortress also served as an elevated observation post for signs of public disturbance in the Temple Courts. The Temple priests' leaders formed a significant part of the Sanhedrin, the Great Council of the nation of Israel that met in the Temple's Hall of Hewn Stones. They had legal authority over Temple Mount and the immediately surrounding area.

The Sadducees were the ruling part of the Jewish priesthood and took their name from Zadok, who was a pupil of Antigonus Sochaeus, a president of the Sanhedrin and a descendant of Aaron.

The name Zadok is derived from the Hebrew *'ṣāḏaq'*, meaning 'just'. He had taught the duty of serving God disinterestedly, without the hope of reward or the fear of punishment. The resultant highly influential priestly sect became one of the three main branches of Judean Jewry (along with the Pharisees and the Essenes).

They held only to the five books of Moses as being authoritative and believed that there was no resurrection, angel nor spirit and also that the soul of man perished with the body.

They were less numerous than the Pharisees, but this was compensated for by their wealth and standing in society as the main Temple guardians. They did not generally seek high office, although several of them were advanced to the office of high priesthood, especially after the award of that office was taken over by the occupying Romans as a political appointment in order to facilitate control over the Judeans.

The Apostles, in common with the Pharisees, offended against the Sadducee's view that there was no bodily resurrection, and furthermore were neither qualified nor legally authorized to teach in the Temple Courts (unlike their *'didaskalôs'* master the Rabbi Jesus). Consequently the priests had the Apostles arrested and imprisoned to await trial the following morning.

In the meantime, over 5,000 people believed Peter's message, supported by the clear healing miracle.

4:5-7 'On the next day, their rulers and elders and scribes were gathered together in Jerusalem; and Annas the high priest was there, and Caiaphas and John and Alexander, and all who were of high-priestly descent. When they had placed them in the center, they began to inquire, "By what power, or in what name, have you done this?"'

Obviously concerned that, having gone to great lengths to finally have Jesus executed, this new Nazarene sect might still have life in it, the Sanhedrin assemble their biggest legal guns to try and browbeat the Apostles into submission. A miracle had undoubtedly occurred, but by what legal right had these unschooled Galileans performed it?

Jesus had instructed his disciples to rely on the Holy Spirit rather than simply their own understanding (Luke 12:12). The priests' insistence that they be given the name of the person through whom the miracle had occurred is met by Peter with extreme clarity, the very well known name of Y'shuah from Nazareth.

The Sanhedrin would have been well aware of the many amazing miracles that Jesus had performed within their own jurisdiction around the Temple, so, frankly, it was just business as usual!

4:11-12 '"He is the stone which was rejected by you, the builders, but which became the chief cornerstone. And there is salvation in no one else; for there is no other name under heaven that has been given among men by which we must be saved."'

Peter then provides a reminder of the order of importance in God's economy.

The Temple in which the Sanhedrin's council room was located had been built by 1000 Jewish Priests, most likely under the training and direction of devout *tektons* such as Joseph, Jesus' father.

As Joseph's firstborn son, Jesus shared equality of societal status with his architect 'earthly' father. And because the builder of the house was proverbially held to have more honour than the house (Hebrews 3:3), both Jesus and Joseph could legitimately claim to be 'greater than the Temple' (Matthew 12:6), whereas the priests had merely been, at best, the builders labouring in a trained, skilled fashion under tekton oversight.

The original cornerstone of Herod's Temple is now in the care of the Jerusalem Museum. It is beveled and weighs approximately 500 tons, dwarfing the many other very large stones used in the Temple's construction process. The stones were provided for the original temple by Solomon's ally, King Hiram of Tyre (1 Kings 5:18), and the most important of all from a structural engineering perspective was the cornerstone (the capstone), referred to by the prophet Isaiah:

'Therefore thus says the Lord God, 'Behold, I am laying in Zion a stone, a tested stone, a costly cornerstone for the foundation, firmly placed. He who believes in it will not be disturbed.' (Isaiah 28:16).

One particular stone block that Hiram, King of Tyre, had provided was so large and unusual in shape that the builders could not initially see a way to incorporate it, and so rejected it. To them it became a 'stumbling stone', as Isaiah had prophesied:

'It is the Lord of hosts whom you should regard as holy, and he shall be your fear, and he shall be your dread. Then he shall become a sanctuary; but to both the houses of Israel, a stone to strike and a rock to stumble over, and a snare and a trap for the inhabitants of Jerusalem. Many will stumble over them, then they will fall and be broken; they will even be snared and caught.' (Isaiah 8:13-15).

Joseph and other devout Judean tektons had personally selected the 500 ton stone that would serve as the capstone for Herod's Temple. The work of the tekton is also clearly described within the work of the Trinity at the creation of the world:

Job 38:1-6 'Then the Lord answered Job out of the whirlwind and said, "Who is this that darkens counsel by words without knowledge? Now gird up your loins like a man, and I will ask you, and you instruct me! Where were you when I laid the foundation of the earth? Tell me, if you have understanding, who set its measurements? Since you know! Or who stretched the [*measuring*] line on it? On what were its bases sunk? Or who laid its **cornerstone** (*Hebrew*: '*pinnah eben*') when the morning stars sang together and all the sons of God shouted for joy?"

4:13-14 'Now as they observed the confidence of Peter and John and understood that they were uneducated and untrained men, they were amazed, and began to recognize them as having been with Jesus. And seeing the man who had been healed standing with them, they had nothing to say in reply.'

'Uneducated' is *'agrammatoi'* – 'unlettered' in a formal higher scholastic capacity, in direct contrast to their master Jesus who is described as 'learned' (John 7:15), having graduated from Bet Midrash in the Temple.

Having so impressed the Doctors of Torah in Bet Midrash at age 12 (Luke 2:41-52), and graduated from there into public rabbinic ministry at age 30 Jesus had all the rabbinic teaching privileges that his disciples did not have. It was this lack of formal rabbinic training that gave rise to the Apostles' arrest for unlawful 'teaching' within the Sanhedrin's legal Temple Mount jurisdiction.

4:15-18 'But when they had ordered them to leave the Council, they began to confer with one another, saying, "What shall we do with these men? For the fact that a noteworthy miracle has taken place through them is apparent to all who live in Jerusalem, and we cannot deny it. But so that it will not spread any further among the people, let us warn them to speak no longer to any man in this name." And when they had summoned them, they commanded them not to speak or teach at all in the name of Jesus.

Having been silenced by the confidence of 'unlearned' Peter, the Sanhedrin now tries to exercise their legal authority upon the Apostles as a group to silence them.

4:19-20 'But Peter and John answered and said to them, "Whether it is right in the sight of God to give heed to you rather than to God, you be the judge; for we cannot stop speaking about what we have seen and heard."'

The Spirit filled and highly faith filled and confident followers of Jesus reply using sarcasm and Jewish humour. They commit themselves to being the 'witnesses' that Jesus had spoken about (Acts 1:8).

4:21-22 'When they had threatened them further, they let them go (finding no basis on which to punish them) on account of the people, because they were all glorifying God for what had happened; for the man was more than forty years old on whom this miracle of healing had been performed.'

Forty was the minimum age of Jewish legally valid independent personal testimony. Together with the crystal clear evidence of the physical miracle and the ecstatic reaction of the Temple crowds, the Sanhedrin were left without a leg to stand on.

4:23-26 'When they had been released, they went to their own companions and reported all that the chief priests and the elders had said to them. And when they heard this, they lifted their voices to God with one accord and said, "O Lord, it is you who made the heaven and the earth and the sea, and all that is in them who by the

Holy Spirit, through the mouth of our father David your servant, said, 'Why did the Gentiles rage, and the peoples devise futile things? The kings of the earth took their stand, and the rulers were gathered together, against the Lord and against his Christ.'"

The reaction of the church in Jerusalem to the Apostles' release is one of praise, singing Psalm 146:5-7 'God, who made heaven and earth, the sea and all that is in them; who keeps faith forever, who executes justice for the oppressed; who gives food to the hungry. The Lord sets the prisoners free.'

They continue their Spirit inspired quotations with Psalm 2:1 'Why are the nations in uproar, and the peoples devising a vain thing?' Use of Scripture in prayer, and especially, the Psalms, was a hallmark of the early Messianic Jewish congregations.

4:27-31 'For truly in this city there were gathered together against your holy servant Jesus, whom you anointed, both Herod and Pontius Pilate, along with the Gentiles and the peoples of Israel, to do whatever your hand and your purpose predestined to occur. "And now, Lord, take note of their threats, and grant that your bond-servants may speak your word with all confidence, while you extend your hand to heal, and signs and wonders take place through the name of your holy servant Jesus." And when they had prayed, the place where they had gathered together was shaken, and they were all filled with the Holy Spirit and began to speak the word of God with boldness.'

Their Spirit-inspired prayer requests God grant them confidence. This is *'parrēsias'*, meaning 'out-spokeness', or a 'bold frankness in publicity and blunt speaking.' The supernatural healings and miracles belonged to God, while the commission to declare the anointed Gospel message belonged to the church.

God was evidently blessed by their praise and prayer, sending another minor earthquake, and a repeat of their recent Pentecost experience. The outworking of that was the *'parrēsias'* for which they had just prayed.

4:32-35 'And the congregation of those who believed were of one heart and soul; and not one of them claimed that anything belonging to him was his own, but all things were common property to them. And with great power the apostles were giving testimony to the resurrection of the Lord Jesus, and abundant grace was upon them all. For there was not a needy person among them, for all who were owners of land or houses would sell them and bring the proceeds of the sales and lay them at the apostles' feet, and they would be distributed to each as any had need.'

'Congregation' here is *'plēthous'*, actually meaning a 'multitude' (of people), who, as Acts 2:45-46 shows, are practicing a radical version of common life, consequential to the extraordinarily high level of grace being experienced.

The power of God was flowing, but unfortunately human sin would soon rear its head.

4:36-37 'Now Joseph, a Levite of Cyprian birth, who was also called Barnabas by the apostles (which translated means Son of Encouragement), and who owned a tract of land, sold it and brought the money and laid it at the apostles' feet.'

Levites were legally prohibited from personal ownership of land (Deuteronomy 12:12, Joshua 14:4), and it may well be that the Holy Spirit reminded and convicted Joseph/Barnabas of this Scriptural truth, causing him to align his priorities with God's word and the prevailing move of the Holy Spirit.

Sadly not everyone was as sensitive to the Spirit's promptings...

Chapter 5

5:1-5 'But a man named Ananias, with his wife Sapphira, sold a piece of property, and kept back some of the price for himself, with his wife's full knowledge, and bringing a portion of it, he laid it at the apostles' feet. But Peter said, "Ananias, why has Satan filled your heart to lie to the Holy Spirit and to keep back some of the price of the land? "While it remained unsold, did it not remain your own? And after it was sold, was it not under your control? Why is it that you have conceived this deed in your heart? You have not lied to men but to God." And as he heard these words, Ananias fell down and breathed his last; and great fear came over all who heard of it. The young men got up and covered him up, and after carrying him out, they buried him.'

'But.' Others with less pure motives than Barnabas decided to get on the property-selling charitable wagon and so portray themselves in a flattering light to the rest of the church, in direct contradiction to Jesus' teaching about financial giving being 'in secret' (Matthew 6:4) and contrary also to regular Judean rabbinic practice.

Ananias had almost certainly had a prior ongoing and deep-rooted sin issue around deception. God disciplines his people in cycles (Leviticus 26), building up towards judgment over a period of time. Ananias' persistence in serious sin at this critical and formative time in the life of the infant church brought him to the final stage of God's discipline, the removal by God from life on earth. The Apostle Paul would later warn the church at Corinth of similarly serious consequences of sin (1 Corinthians 11:30) in the context of their *'agape'* meals.

5:7-11 'Now there elapsed an interval of about three hours, and his wife came in, not knowing what had happened. And Peter responded to her, "Tell me whether you sold the land for such and such a price?" And she said, "Yes, that was the price." Then Peter said to her, "Why is it that you have agreed together to put the Spirit of the Lord to the test? Behold, the feet of those who have buried your husband are at the door, and they will carry you out as well." And immediately she fell at his feet and breathed her last, and the young men came in and found her dead, and they carried her out and buried her beside her husband. And great fear came over the whole church, and over all who heard of these things.'

Property sales were transacted semi-publicly at the city gates. It is quite possible that one of the many thousand members of the early church had alerted Peter to the deception, however, only the Holy Spirit could have given Peter the revelation concerning Sapphira's impending demise. Jesus had confronted many people about their sinful behaviour without them dropping dead, and Ananias' collapse must have shocked Peter deeply, causing him to seek further divine guidance in prayer.

The overall effect upon the church and their associates is one of a deep supernatural awe (Greek *'phobos'*), leading to the 'esteem' referred to in verse 13.

5:12-13 'At the hands of the apostles many signs and wonders were taking place among the people; and they were all with one accord in Solomon's portico. But none of the rest dared to associate with them; however, the people held them in high esteem.'

The widespread sense of awe that surrounded the new move of the Holy Spirit led to an inevitable separation between believer and unbeliever. The church now consisted of many thousands of people, who had experienced a unity described as 'one accord'. This is *'homothymadón'*- from *'homo'* - 'same' and *'thymos'* - 'passion'. The church was experiencing the fruit of Jesus' own high priestly prayer (John 17), that they would be one, united in mind and purpose, unanimous in deed and purpose, with the Holy Spirit confirming his word in miraculous power.

5:14-16 'And all the more believers in the Lord, multitudes of men and women, were constantly added to their number, to such an extent that they even carried the sick out into the streets and laid them on cots and pallets, so that when Peter came by at least his shadow might fall on any one of them. Also the people from the cities in the vicinity of Jerusalem were coming together, bringing people who were sick or afflicted with unclean spirits, and they were all being healed.'

God himself grows his church. The city of Jerusalem contained many thousands of people who were familiar with the very recent ministry of Jesus in the Temple Courts, and in whose hearts God's Spirit was already at work. The plentiful harvest that Jesus had identified

(Matthew 19: 37-38) was being gathered in by that most reliable of harvest field workers, God himself. Jesus' healing ministry was continuing in the extraordinary way that he had himself foretold: "Truly, truly, I say to you, he who believes in me, the works that I do, he will do also; and greater works than these he will do; because I go to the Father." (John 14:12).

5:17-22 'But the High Priest rose up, along with all his associates (that is the sect of the Saducees), and they were filled with jealousy. They laid hands on the apostles and put them in a public jail. But during the night an angel of the Lord opened the gates of the prison, and taking them out he said, "Go, stand and speak to the people in the temple the whole message of this Life." Upon hearing this, they entered into the temple about daybreak and began to teach.'

Throughout this time of grace and miracles the enemies of the infant church had not been idle. The ruling priestly Sadducees were well aware of the miraculous manifestations of grace that were occurring and were filled with much 'zēlou' - 'heated envy and indignation'. It was a case of: "How dare these common sinners perform miracles! We're much more important than them. How dare they even meet without **our** permission on **our** premises in Solomon's portico!"

And so they exercise their legal authority to have the apostles arrested and locked up in jail. This, however, contradicted the absolute will of God, who simply sent one of his many 'angelos' messenger angels to release them and get them back on track with his perfect and absolute will. This was the continuing of Jesus' ministry of speaking God's word in the Courts of God's house despite the Apostles lack of formal academic accreditation and the anger and disapproval of the Temple's formal priestly custodians.

5:21-23 'Now when the High Priest and his associates came, they called the Council together, even all the Senate of the sons of Israel, and sent orders to the prison house for them to be brought. But the officers who came did not find them in the prison; and they returned and reported back, saying, "We found the prison house locked quite securely and the guards standing at the doors; but when we had opened up, we found no one inside."'

Now well fed and rested, the ruling priests assembled the whole Sanhedrin council (seventy elders) to decide the fate of these troublesome followers of Jesus. But sadly the accused had vanished, leaving no trace of the means of their escape.

5:24-26 'Now when the Captain of the temple guard and the chief priests heard these words, they were greatly perplexed about them as to what would come of this. But someone came and reported to them, "The men whom you put in prison are standing in the temple and teaching the people!" Then the Captain went along with the officers and proceeded to bring them back without violence (for they were afraid of the people, that they might be stoned).'

The Temple Guard (priests trained in soldiery by the occupying Romans), were educated Jews well acquainted with Jesus and his superb teaching abilities. Despite the Apostles blatant repetition of their unlawful teaching of the people, they know better than to interfere with such publically acclaimed holy men. The more senior players among the Priests' opposition are similarly *'diēporoun'* ('greatly perplexed') and at a loss to know what to do.

When the Sanhedrin hear that the apostles are back doing the very thing they have been expressly told not to do, they become fearful rather than angry. Possibly experiencing a dawning understanding that something is going on that is bigger than they can handle, they are certainly cautious of the Temple crowd's notorious proclivity to reactionary religious violence. Many of the crowd would have been from Galilee, short-fused and understandably supportive of both Jesus and the fellow Galileans amongst the apostles.

5:27-32 'When they had brought them, they stood them before the Council. The High Priest questioned them, saying, "We gave you strict orders not to continue teaching in this name, and yet, you have filled Jerusalem with your teaching and intend to bring this man's blood upon us." But Peter and the apostles answered, "We must obey God rather than men. The God of our fathers raised up Jesus, whom you had put to death by hanging him on a cross. He is the one whom God exalted to his right hand as a Prince and a Saviour, to grant repentance to Israel, and forgiveness of sins. And we are witnesses of these things; and so is the Holy Spirit, whom God has given to those who obey him."

The High Priest too, having engineered Jesus' execution (hence 'whom **you** had put to death') is acutely aware of the degree of risk to him and his family in the apostles' teaching. Peter's response is to encapsulate the Gospel message and point to the resurrection (something priests did not believe in) as evidence of who Jesus really was, the promised Messiah.

5:33-34 'But when they heard this, they were cut to the quick and intended to kill them. But a Pharisee named Gamaliel, a teacher of the Law, respected by all the people, stood up in the Council and gave orders to put the men outside for a short time.'

The idea that God had vindicated Jesus' ministry by raising him from the dead did not please the Sanhedrin and its priestly members who did not believe in bodily resurrection from death, but were certainly sufficiently arrogant to be comfortable with ending human life. 'Cut to the quick/heart' is *'diaprió'* – literally, 'sawn in half' - with anger and indignation.

Enter Gamaliel, a very famous senior Pharisee who **did** believe in resurrection.

The learned grandson of one of Judaism's greatest ever rabbis, Rabbi Hillel (110BC-10AD), Gamaliel was a senior Doctor of Torah/teacher currently overseeing the apostle Paul (Acts 22:3), and one of the 23 Pharisees represented on the Sanhedrin. He was one of only 6 rabbis to ever be given the title 'Rabban' within the religious office of 'Nasi', the highest first century Jewish religious authority. A very wise man (said to possibly later have come to faith in Jesus as Messiah), he first obtained privacy for his counsel. We perhaps have the believing Sanhedrin member Nicodemus to thank for reporting the subsequent dialogue, or possibly Paul himself, who was likely present also.

5:35-39 'And he said to them, "Men of Israel, take care what you propose to do with these men. For some time ago Theudas rose up, claiming to be somebody, and a group of about four hundred men joined up with him. But he was killed, and all who followed him were dispersed and came to nothing. After this man, Judas of Galilee rose up in the days of the census and drew away some people after him; he too perished, and all those who followed him were scattered. So in the present case, I say to you, stay away from these men and let them alone, for if this plan or action is of men, it will be overthrown; but if it is of God, you will not be able to overthrow them; or else you may even be found fighting against God."'

The master rabbi recommends masterly inactivity. He cites two recent examples of the (frequent) religious uprisings against the pagan Roman military occupations that had fizzled out following their leaders' deaths, and recommends a wise 'wait and see' approach.

5:40-42 'They took his advice; and after calling the apostles in, they flogged them and ordered them not to speak in the name of Jesus, and then released them. So they went on their way from the presence of the Council, rejoicing that they had been considered worthy to suffer shame for his name. And every day, in the Temple and from house to house, they kept right on teaching and preaching Jesus as the Christ.'

The Jews judicial punishment of flogging (Greek: 'derô') was very different to the scourging *(mastizo')* practiced by the Romans which Jesus had experienced (Matthew 27:26).

The Roman flogging was done with a *'phragelloo'*, which Paul was threatened with in Acts 22:25, an instrument of torture with frequently fatal consequences.

Floggings as prescribed by Jewish law were relatively benign by comparison and consisted of being beaten with a padded wooden paddle type implement 39 times, divided into three lots of thirteen, and distributed between the lower back and the rear of both shoulders. A publicly humiliating and painful experience certainly, but not one designed to maim or kill.

The Apostles treat the punishment's (*'atimazô'* - 'shame') as a badge of honour, joyfully choosing to not behave silently as instructed by the Sanhedrin, but rather, *'euaggelizô'* - 'announcing the Good News' about Messiah both publically in the Temple and privately in people's homes just as they had been continually doing up to that point.

Chapter 6

6:1-6 'Now at this time while the disciples were increasing in number, a complaint arose on the part of the Hellenistic Jews against the native Hebrews, because their widows were being overlooked in the daily serving of food. So the twelve summoned the congregation of the disciples and said, "It is not desirable for us to neglect the word of God in order to serve tables. Therefore, brethren, select from among you seven men of good reputation, full of the Spirit and of wisdom, whom we may put in charge of this task. But we will devote ourselves to prayer and to the ministry of the word." The statement found approval with the whole congregation; and they chose Stephen, a man full of faith and of the Holy Spirit, and Philip, Prochorus, Nicanor, Timon, Parmenas and Nicolas, a proselyte from Antioch. And these they brought before the apostles; and after praying, they laid their hands on them.'

Trouble is now closer to home. The multi-ethnic infant church had some residual prejudices that surfaced over something as basic as food. The Hellenists were Jews whose first language was Greek rather than the local Judean Aramaic. Widows without any immediate family to support them were cared for by the wider community, but some racial discrimination started to occur in the vital area of food distribution.

The Apostles were naturally occupied with teaching the word of God and with prayer. They take the eminently sensible step of appointing men to focus on areas of practical service, thereby freeing them to focus on the ministry-service of God's word. The Greek here is *'diakonia'*, meaning the menial task type of 'service', and from which the word 'deacon' is derived. The criteria were a simple and early form of the human and spiritual qualifications detailed in the later Pastoral Epistles of Paul and Peter.

And so the first person to 'love Jesus unto death' is appointed. The names of the men chosen with Stephen were, like him, indicative of native Greek speaking Jews who were therefore able to more easily bridge the ethnic divide and so help the Greek-speaking widows. 'Laying on of hands' was the established public sign of designating spiritual authority (Numbers 27:18) and had become a part of the Jews' formal *'semikha'* rabbinic ordination process.

6:7 'The word of God kept on spreading; and the number of the disciples continued to increase greatly in Jerusalem, and a great many of the priests were becoming obedient to the faith.'

The) word of God is, by nature, 'living and active' (Hebrews 4:12), and so, like yeast, is behaving in its usual way and increasing ('spreading'). While the upper echelons of the priesthood had become corrupted by extreme wealth and the political machinations of the occupying Romans, many were devout men who had heard and seen the ministry of the Lord Jesus and knew of Gethsemane's empty tomb. Large numbers of them believed the gospel and were added to the infant church.

'Obedient' is *'hypēkouon'* ('to hear under') indicating a transference of their spiritual allegiance from the Sanhedrin ruling council to Jesus and his apostles.

6:8-12 'And Stephen, full of grace and power, was performing great wonders and signs among the people. But some men from what was called the Synagogue of the Freedmen, including both Cyrenians and Alexandrians, and some from Cilicia and Asia, rose up and argued with Stephen. But they were unable to cope with the wisdom and the Spirit with which he was speaking. Then they secretly induced men to say, "We have heard him speak blasphemous words against Moses and against God." And they stirred up the people, the elders and the scribes, and they came up to him and dragged him away and brought him before the Council.'

Stephen's ministry, so reminiscent of the Lord Jesus' own life, inevitably attracted serious spiritual opposition. 'Freedman' is *'libertinōn'*, a Latin word indicating a subgrouping of Jews who had been captured en masse by the Roman army and then released and permitted to settle in various territories with some Roman privileges. Philo (in *'Legat'*) describes this practice as having been conducted by the Roman military commander Pompey (106-48BC), and a similar practice is known to have occurred under the Egyptian ruler Ptolemy 1 (367-282BC).

These particular Jews hailed from Libya, Egypt and Asia, all under Roman rule at the time. Cilicia, on the Mediterranean seacoast, was the home of Saul of Tarsus, and it is likely that this brilliant and zealous disciple of Gamaliel was active in picking this particular doctrinal fight with Stephen as he presided over his subsequent execution. Unable to win the legal argument, false witnesses are appointed alleging blasphemy, a capital offense, and once again the Sanhedrin's lethal services are required.

6:3-15 'They put forward false witnesses who said, "This man incessantly speaks against this holy place and the Law; for we have heard him say that this Nazarene, Jesus, will destroy this place and alter the customs which Moses handed down to us." And fixing their gaze on him, all who were sitting in the Council saw his face like the face of an angel.'

The old 'destroy this Temple' (John 2:19 and Matthew 26:61) line resurfaces again. The devil is not noted for his original ideas, and since it had usefully contributed to Jesus' conviction it is again rolled out as evidence of alleged religious subversion.

Meanwhile Stephen is so full of the Spirit of God that his physical countenance takes on an angelic appearance, presumably shining with God's glory in the same way Moses' face had shone following his encounter with the second person of the Trinity on Mount Sinai (Exodus 34:29). The priests did not believe in the existence of angels, but the Pharisees on the Sanhedrin most certainly did (Acts 23:8).

Chapter 7

7:1-8 'The high priest said, "Are these things so?" And he said, "Hear me, brethren and fathers! The God of glory appeared to our father Abraham when he was in Mesopotamia, before he lived in Haran, and said to him, 'Leave your country and your relatives, and come into the land that I will show you.' Then he left the land of the Chaldeans and settled in Haran. From there, after his father died, God had him move to this country in which you are now living. But he gave him no inheritance in it, not even a foot of ground, and yet, even when he had no child, he promised that he would give it to him as a possession and to his descendants after him. But God spoke to this effect, that his descendants would be aliens in a foreign land, and that they would be enslaved and mistreated for four hundred years. And to whatever nation to which they will be in bondage I myself will judge, said God, and after that they will come out and serve me in this place.' And he gave him the covenant of circumcision; and so Abraham became the father of Isaac, and circumcised him on the eighth day; and Isaac became the father of Jacob, and Jacob of the twelve patriarchs.'"

Stephen commences his defense respectfully, in traditional fashion, by reminding the Sanhedrin, which may well have numbered Saul of Tarsus (the likely primary source of the speech content for Luke's use). He reminds them of their patriarch Abraham's origins as a foreigner living in a foreign land prior to the call of God coming to him.

The Sanhedrin Council may well have looked down on Stephen as a non-native Hebrew speaker, but Stephen's wisdom, combined with the supernatural anointing of the Holy Spirit, would soon prove too much for them.

7:9-10 'The patriarchs became jealous of Joseph and sold him into Egypt. Yet God was with him, and rescued him from all his afflictions, and granted him favour and wisdom in the sight of Pharaoh, king of Egypt, and he made him governor over Egypt and all his household.'

Stephen introduces another stranger in a strange land. Having been betrayed and sold into slavery by his brothers, Joseph was forced to live as a Hebrew in the hostile land of Egypt where God prospered him in spite of the adversity.

7:11-16 '"Now a famine came over all Egypt and Canaan, and great affliction with it, and our fathers could find no food. But when Jacob heard that there was grain in Egypt, he sent our fathers there the first time. On the second visit Joseph made himself known to his mbrothers and Joseph's family was disclosed to Pharaoh. Then Joseph sent word and invited Jacob his father and all his relatives to come to him, seventy-five persons in all. And Jacob went down to Egypt and there he and our fathers died. From there they were removed to Shechem and laid in the tomb which Abraham had purchased for a sum of money from the sons of Hamor In Shechem."'

Joseph had a hidden role in securing the feeding and survival of the patriarchs and their families, and hence the lineage of the people of God through whom Messiah would come. Once again foreigners and foreign places such as Egypt and the Canaanites of Shechem feature as having great importance in the provenance and plans of God.

7:17-22 "'But as the time of the promise was approaching which God had assured to Abraham, the people increased and multiplied in Egypt, until there arose another king over Egypt who knew nothing about Joseph. It was he who took shrewd advantage of our race and mistreated our fathers so that they would expose their infants and they would not survive. It was at this time that Moses was born; and he was lovely in the sight of God, and he was nurtured three months in his father's home. And after he had been set outside, Pharaoh's daughter took him away and nurtured him as her own son. Moses was educated in all the learning of the Egyptians, and he was a man of power in words and deeds.'"

Messiah was to be 'a prophet like Moses' (Deuteronomy 18:15). Moses grew up in a hidden capacity (a Hebrew but widely believed to be the son of Pharaoh's daughter) in the place of Egyptian higher learning and wisdom. Stephen is drawing a clear comparison with Jesus ('a man of power in words and deeds'), who had emerged aged 30 into public ministry from the Temple's place of higher learning (Bet Midrash) to conduct an initially rejected ministry of salvation in a similar way to that of Moses, who was also rejected.

7:23-29 "'But when he was approaching the age of forty, it entered his mind to visit his brethren, the sons of Israel. And when he saw one of them being treated unjustly, he defended him and took vengeance for the oppressed by striking down the Egyptian. And he supposed that his brethren understood that God was granting them deliverance through him, but they did not understand. On the following day he appeared to them as they were fighting together, and he tried to reconcile them in peace, saying, 'Men, you are brethren, why do you injure one another?' But the one who was injuring his neighbour pushed him away, saying, 'Who made you a ruler and judge over us? You do not mean to kill us as you killed the Egyptian yesterday, do you?' At this remark, Moses fled and became an alien in the land of Midian, where he became the father of two sons.'"

Moses' rank as a prince in Egypt stood for nothing with his fellow Hebrews, who were in ignorance of his true identity and his God-given intention to free them from their servitude.

7:30-34 "'After forty years had passed, an angel appeared to him in the wilderness of Mount Sinai, in the flame of a burning thorn bush. When Moses saw it, he marveled at the sight; and as he approached to look more closely, there came the voice of the Lord: 'I am the God of your fathers, the God of Abraham and Isaac and Jacob.' Moses shook with fear and would not venture to look. But the Lord said to him, 'Take off the sandals from your feet, for the place on which you are standing is holy ground. I have certainly seen the oppression of my people in Egypt and have heard their groans, and I have come down to rescue them; come now, and I will send you to Egypt."

Moses was sent back into a place of hostility toward him just as Jesus had frequently returned to the hostile

Sanhedrin's domain (Temple Mount) in the fulfillment of God the Father's salvation mission and purpose. In Jesus' incarnation God himself 'had come down to rescue'.

7:35-43 "'This Moses whom they disowned, saying, 'Who made you a ruler and a judge?' is the one whom God sent to be both a ruler and a deliverer with the help of the angel who appeared to him in the thorn bush. This man led them out, performing wonders and signs in the land of Egypt and in the Red Sea and in the wilderness for forty years. This is the Moses who said to the sons of Israel, 'God will raise up for you a prophet like me from among your brethren.' This is the one who was in the congregation in the wilderness together with the angel who was speaking to him on Mount Sinai, and who was with our fathers; and he received living oracles to pass on to you. Our fathers were unwilling to be obedient to him, but repudiated him and in their hearts turned back to Egypt, saying to Aaron, 'Make us Gods who will go before us; as for this Moses who led us out of the land of Egypt – we do not know what happened to him.' At that time they made a calf and brought a sacrifice to the idol, and were rejoicing in the works of their hands. But God turned away and delivered them up to serve the host of heaven; as it is written in the book of the prophets, 'It was no to me that you offered victims and sacrifices forty years in the wilderness, was it, O house of Israel? You also took along the tabernacle of Molech and the star of the god Rompha, the images which you made to worship. I also will remove you beyond Babylon.'"

Israel had a long track record of involvement in the evil and idolatrous practices of their neighbours. Even King

Solomon had built a temple to Molech on the Mount of Olives for his many foreign wives (1 Kings 11:7-8).

'Rompha' (or 'Remphan') is the Egyptian term for Saturn (Hebrew: *'Chiun'*), another idolatrous influence contributing to God's eventual judgment of Israel manifested in the forced exile to Babylon c. 600BC.

7:44-50 "'Our fathers had the tabernacle of testimony in the wilderness, just as he who spoke to Moses directed him to make it according to the pattern which he had seen. And having received it in their turn, our fathers brought it in with Joshua upon dispossessing the nations whom God drove out before our fathers, until the time of David. David found favour in God's sight, and asked that he might find a dwelling place for the God of Jacob. But it was Solomon who built a house for him. However, the Most High does not dwell in houses made by human hands; as the prophet says: 'Heaven is my throne and earth is my footstool, what kind of house will you build for me?' says the Lord, 'or what place is there for my repose? Was it not my hand that made all these things?"

To further emphasize the fact that he is really speaking to them about Jesus of Nazareth, Stephen introduces a specifically *'tekton'* reference. The 'pattern' for the Tabernacle was a detailed construction plan that the Heavenly Creator-Architect had given to Moses on Mount Sinai. Temple construction is being referred to, in the same way Peter had done to these very same men in Acts 4:11. The Temple of Herod, where the Sanhedrin met, was a source of immense pride (and wealth) to them, and they would have been well aware of the role that Jesus' devout *'tekton'* father Joseph had played in training and overseeing the one thousand priests that had built it. But God himself was, of course, much greater than his Temple-house.

7:51-53 '"You men who are stiff-necked and uncircumcised in heart and ears are always resisting the Holy Spirit; you are doing just as your fathers did. Which one of the prophets did your fathers not persecute? They killed those who had previously announced the coming of the Righteous One, whose betrayers and murderers you have now become; you who received the law as ordained by angels, and yet did not keep it."'

The gloves finally come off, because the Sanhedrin is behaving just like their corrupt and rebellious forefathers. Having had a long track record of murdering prophets, the current generation of Israel's rulers have gone one better and unlawfully put to death the Messiah himself!

7:54-60 'Now when they heard this, they were cut to the quick, and they began gnashing their teeth at him. But being full of the Holy Spirit, he gazed intently into heaven and saw the glory of God, and Jesus standing at the right hand of God; and he said, "Behold, I see the heavens opened up and the Son of Man standing at the right hand of God." But they cried out with a loud voice, and covered their ears and rushed at him with one impulse. When they had driven him out of the city, they began stoning him; and the witnesses laid aside their robes at the feet of a young man named Saul. They went on stoning Stephen as he called on the Lord and said, "Lord Jesus, receive my spirit!" Then falling on his knees, he cried out with a loud voice, "Lord, do not hold this sin against them!" Having said this, he fell asleep.'

Extreme rage can lead to involuntary clenching of the jaw muscles, accompanied by a scowling biting movement of the mouth. The Sanhedrin heard themselves described by Stephen as traitors towards God and murderers towards his messengers and were 'cut' (*diaprió*) to the heart – literally 'sawn in two' with anger and indignation. This is the exact same response that the Sanhedrin had had towards the apostles in Acts 5:33, only on this occasion there is apparently no Gamaliel present or willing to defuse it.

The vision of Jesus standing at God's right hand is the final straw that tips the Sanhedrin over the edge of reason and into a frantic, rage-maddened and illegally precipitate summary execution.

Once again, Dr Luke's editorial movie camera swings around to focus in on Saul of Tarsus, almost certainly Luke's source of detail and currently one of the villains but soon to be the hero of this narrative written by the superb first century historian Luke for the benefit of Caesar's Court in Rome.

Saul was acting in an official legal capacity as the Sanhedrin's overseer in the discharge of their own powers of summary execution of Stephen for his apparent blasphemy in proclaiming Jesus as Messiah and standing in authority at God's right hand. Stephen's faith-filled manner of dying would leave a strong impression on Saul.

Saul would later (Acts 26:10) say to King Agrippa that he 'cast his vote' in favour of the death sentence for the early Jewish followers of Messiah. This is a reference to the Sanhedrin's practice of voting by literally casting white or black pebbles, the different pebbles' colours representing the member's consent or dissent for the motion in question.

The Jewish Talmud (*Hagigah* 2:11 and *Bezah* 2:4) records this to have been the usual means by which decisions on both judicial matters and questions of religious interpretation were collectively taken.

Meanwhile Stephen, deep in personal and others-focused prayer, is quietly becoming the infant church's first martyr.

Chapter 8

8:1-3 'Saul was in hearty agreement with putting him to death. And on that day a great persecution began against the church in Jerusalem, and they were all scattered throughout the regions of Judea and Samaria, except the apostles. Some devout men buried Stephen, and made loud lamentation over him. But Saul began ravaging the church, entering house after house, and dragging off men and women, he would put them in prison.'

The Greek for 'hearty agreement' is *'syneudokéō'*, from *'sýn'*- 'to identify with', and *'eudokéō'* – 'seems good'. Saul's official standing is further evidenced by verse 3; he clearly possessed Sanhedrin arrest warrants from the High Priest to whom he would have been personally known as a vehement Pharisaic opponent of this infant Messianic splinter group from religious mainstream Judaism, which became known as 'The Way' (Acts 19:23).

The twelve apostles evidently enjoyed some form of protection or favour with the Sanhedrin, perhaps still consequential to the very senior Pharisee Gamaliel's recent advice that they be left alone.

From a medical/psychological standpoint, Saul's extremely ferocious behaviour is best explained by the psychology of **betrayal**. Jesus had certainly been the most outstanding (and officially legally qualified) exponent of Torah/Scripture ever to grace the Temple Courts and its resident rabbinic schooling system.

As such, Saul, a slightly junior contemporary of Jesus', would have naturally felt a desire to be personally instructed by Jesus and would have inevitably felt bemused by Jesus' choice of relatively unschooled and somewhat uncouth Galileans as his disciples. Northern fishermen such as Simon Peter were not usually prominent among the elite religious intellectuals of Bet Midrash.

Jesus' apparent theological swerve to taking upon himself God's unspeakable name and the divine role of forgiving others' sins, saddled further by intentional Sabbath breaking, would have been witnessed by Saul with, at first, disbelief, rapidly followed by intense outrage and a sense of deeply personal betrayal of the things of God that the highly religious Jews held so dear.

Saul/Paul's academic religious knowledge had taken him on the long journey, aged 13, from Tarsus in Cilicia, in modern day south-eastern Turkey, to Jerusalem. Paul had been invited to enroll, at a cost, in Rabbi Gamaliel's Torah school, a great honour for any Jew and especially one who lived outside the land of Israel.

This in turn points to Paul's family background, which would have been not only extremely devout but also wealthy and with a high social standing from the wider Roman perspective.

This had occurred a few years after Jesus' own arrival in the Temple's Torah/Scripture University/school of 'Bet Midrash', the well recognised (genius) son of Joseph, the senior Temple *'tekton'*. Paul would later (Acts 26:11) describe himself as having been 'driven mad with rage' by Jesus and his devout Jewish followers' apparent U-turn from the well worn path of ancient rabbinic traditions and into apparent blasphemies.

Hence Saul's extreme and very violent responses. The Greek for 'ravaging' is *'elymaineto'* - literally 'the havoc and devastation caused by a wild beast'. Saul's behaviour is out of control, driven by a madness of rage fuelled by a sense of personal and religious betrayal at the deepest psychological level. Believing that he is serving God, he commits acts of violence against the dispersed Judean disciples., imprisoning them and hounding them.

8:4-8 'Therefore, those who had been scattered went about preaching the word. Philip went down to the city of Samaria and began proclaiming Christ to them. The crowds with one accord were giving attention to what was said by Philip, as they heard and saw the signs which he was performing. For in the case *of* many who had unclean spirits, they were coming out of them shouting with a loud voice; and many who had been paralyzed and lame were healed. So there was much rejoicing in that city.'

Meanwhile, the Holy Spirit is turning the very negative and violent persecution into a force for good as the compulsorily dispersed disciples carry the gospel message as seed with them to many new places.

Samaria had historically been viewed as being off limits to the devout Jewish descendants of those who had returned from the forced exile in Babylon. They found that those (non-Judean Jews) who had been left behind to cultivate the land had inter-married with their heathen neighbours, virtually abandoning both the study and the therefore the correct rabbinic practice of Torah law.

The possibly rather more cosmopolitan and Greek speaking Philip had no such prejudicial inhibitions, and, led by the indwelling Holy Spirit, goes there and preaches the Gospel to them, in obedience to Jesus' direct instruction (Acts 1:8).

Naturally, signs and wonders follow. Demons are evicted and the paralyzed find themselves now supernaturally able to walk. Luke employs a degree of understatement in his description of the ecstatic response from those who had previously only heard a distant rumour of such miraculous but now apparently commonplace happenings in neighbouring Judea.

The Greek text rendered here as 'much rejoicing' is *'polýs chara'*, literally meaning 'much ongoing joy', indicating the recurring nature of a very unprejudiced God's direct interventions in their lives.

8:9-13 'Now there was a man named Simon, who formerly was practicing magic in the city and astonishing the people of Samaria, claiming to be someone great; and they all, from smallest to greatest, were giving attention to him, saying, "This man is what is called the Great Power of God." And they were giving him attention because he had for a long time astonished them with his magic arts. But when they believed Philip preaching the good news about the kingdom of God and the name of Jesus Christ, they were being baptized, men and women alike. Even Simon himself believed; and after being baptized, he continued on with Philip, and as he observed signs and great miracles taking place, he was constantly amazed.'

The Samaritan's most recent previous experiences of the supernatural had been of a different nature altogether. Simon; whom the first century Jewish Roman historian Josephus Flavius ('Antiquities' 20,7,2) also described as a 'magus' (after the practices of the foreign spiritual and political advisors to the Persians (Daniel 1:20). Simon had apparently studied philosophy at the University of Alexandria in Egypt before establishing his reputation as a 'magician' in Samaria.

Like the advisors to the Egyptian Pharaohs (Exodus 7:11) they practiced a counterfeit type of magic that was both powerful and demonically extremely deceptive, but was to prove to be no match for the Holy Spirit.

When the truly divine 'great power of God' arrived in Samaria, Simon instantly recognized it as the genuine article and coveted it as an ungodly means of gaining even greater control over others. Sadly, this errant desire persisted even after he had come to a degree of faith himself, even being baptized, having been astounded by witnessing first hand the powerful miracles being performed by the evangelist Philip.

8:14-17 'Now when the apostles in Jerusalem heard that Samaria had received the word of God, they sent them Peter and John, who came down and prayed for them that they might receive the Holy Spirit. For he had not yet fallen upon any of them; they had simply been baptized in the name of the Lord Jesus. Then they began laying their hands on them, and they were receiving the Holy Spirit.'

The outpouring of the Holy Spirit, as had been experienced by the disciples in Jerusalem on the day of Pentecost, had not yet become something established as a general form of ongoing grace of to be available to all believers (Colossians 1:9).

It was evidently something still viewed as requiring the personal input of the apostles, who duly cast off any reservations about ministering to the legally unclean 'half-Jew' Samaritans and faithfully came in answer to Philip's news of this fresh work of the Spirit.

The laying on of hands was the commonly recognized Jewish means of prayer and formal rabbinic impartation by and of spiritual authority, which God duly blessed in outwardly visible ways.

8:18-24 'Now when Simon saw that the Spirit was bestowed through the laying on of the apostles' hands, he offered them money, saying, "Give this authority to me as well, so that everyone on whom I lay my hands may receive the Holy Spirit." But Peter said to him, "May your silver perish with you, because you thought you could obtain the gift of God with money! "You have no part or portion in this matter, for your heart is not right before God. "Therefore repent of this wickedness of yours, and pray the Lord that, if possible, the intention of your heart may be forgiven you. "For I see that you are in the gall of bitterness and in the bondage of iniquity." But Simon answered and said, "Pray to the Lord for me yourselves, so that nothing of what you have said may come upon me.'

The idea that this foreign 'magus' Simon could somehow buy his way to God and his gifts was absolutely abhorrent to the apostles. What Simon asked for was the *'exousia'* of the gift of God's Spirit, the 'authority, power and influence' over others that Simon had had an illegitimate measure of (one very corrupted spiritually), before meeting the one true God.

Instead, Peter promises him *'apóleia'*, the 'eternal ruin/loss of well-being' that comes from being cut off from God. This is quite a promise for a baptized 'believer'!

But where sin abounds, there grace also abounds (Romans 5:20), and Peter's challenge to Simon is that he practice the 'change his thinking' that is repentance and be forgiven.

He was then able to break free from his poisonous bitterness and his enslavement to unrighteous and controlling behaviour, and be 'forgiven' (literally let off) by God for his wrongdoing.

8:25 'So, when they had solemnly testified and spoken the word of the Lord, they started back to Jerusalem, and were preaching the gospel to many villages of the Samaritans.'

Simon having been duly sorted out, the apostles make the most of their return journey to Jerusalem by proclaiming the gospel's 'good news' of Jesus' victory over sin and death to those Samaritan villages that hadn't had the benefit of a personal visit from the Messiah himself.

8:26-31 'But an angel of the Lord spoke to Philip saying, "Get up and go south to the road that descends from Jerusalem to Gaza." (This is a desert road.) So he got up and went; and there was an Ethiopian eunuch, a court official of Candace, queen of the Ethiopians, who was in charge of all her treasure; and he had come to Jerusalem to worship, and he was returning and sitting in his chariot, and was reading the prophet Isaiah. Then the Spirit said to Philip, "Go up and join this chariot." Philip ran up and heard him reading Isaiah the prophet, and said, "Do you understand what you are reading?" And he said, "Well, how could I, unless someone guides me?" And he invited Philip to come up and sit with him.'

Angels conveyed divine messages. Philip is instructed to go south for a divine appointment near Gaza, some 60 miles southwest of Jerusalem to the surrounding 'wilderness'/scrubland there.

On this direct route to Egypt and Ethiopia he saw a stationary chariot in which an Ethiopian sat reading from the scroll of Isaiah the prophet. The man was clearly a wealthy God fearing convert to Judaism (chariots and scrolls were extremely expensive), a Gentile who believed in and followed the God of Israel up to but not including the uncomfortable rite of circumcision. He was also a high-ranking courtier to Candace the queen of Ethiopia.

The Roman historian Pliny ('Natural History' 7, 29) wrote about Ethiopia that: 'Women reigned there under the name of Candace, which name had been transmitted to these queens for many years.' Queen Candace was the sovereign ruler over the North African region of Cush (the region south of Egypt) and Arabia.

The term *'eunouchos'* used by Luke can denote both literal emasculation and can also refer to the local governmental office of chamberlain. Candace's treasurer was returning home to Ethiopia having celebrated a religious festival in Jerusalem and was found by Philip reading from the Septuagint, the commonly circulated Greek translation of the Old Testament. The passage he was reading was Isaiah 53 (verses 7 and 8).

8:32-34 'Now, the passage of Scripture which he was reading was this: 'He was led as a sheep to slaughter;

and as a lamb before its shearer is silent, so he does not open his mouth. In humiliation his judgment was taken away; who will relate his generation? For his life is removed from the earth.' The eunuch answered Philip and said, "Please tell me, of whom does the prophet say this? Of himself or of someone else?"'

The passage had traditionally been held to be referring to the promised Messiah, and so the Holy Spirit had provided Philip with a golden opportunity to share the very recent fulfillment of this prophecy. It is likely that the eunuch was extremely familiar with the scroll of the prophet Isaiah, not least on account of the neighbouring passage in Isaiah 56 concerning 'foreigners' and officials/eunuchs.

Isaiah 56:3-7 'Let not the **foreigner** who has joined himself to the Lord say, "The Lord will surely separate me from his people." Nor let the **eunuch** say, "Behold, I am a dry tree. For thus says the Lord, "To the eunuchs who keep my Sabbaths, and choose what pleases me, and hold fast my covenant, to them I will give in my house and within my walls a memorial, and a name better than that of sons and daughters; I will give them an everlasting name which will not be cut off. Also the foreigners who join themselves to the Lord, to minister to him, and to love the name of the Lord, to be his servants, every one who keeps from profaning the Sabbath and holds fast my covenant. Even those I will bring to my holy mountain and make them joyful in my house of prayer. Their burnt offerings and their sacrifices will be acceptable on my altar; for my house will be called a house of prayer for all the peoples."

Such wonderful promises from the God of Israel to foreign eunuchs must surely have stimulated this Ethiopian's personal interest.

8:35-39 'Then Philip opened his mouth, and beginning from this Scripture he preached Jesus to him. As they went along the road they came to some water; and the eunuch said, "Look! Water! What prevents me from being baptized?" And Philip said, "If you believe with all your heart, you may." And he answered and said, "I believe that Jesus Christ is the Son of God." And he ordered the chariot to stop; and they both went down into the water, Philip as well as the eunuch, and he baptized him. When they came up out of the water, the Spirit of the Lord snatched Philip away; and the eunuch no longer saw him, but went on his way rejoicing.'

Philip now operates under the direct influence and inspiration of the Holy Spirit, moving from the Scripture-based start to an inspired extemporaneous exposition of the Gospel. The Ethiopian believes and his heart is further opened by the Spirit through faith into baptism by immersion, whereupon mission accomplished, God supernaturally moves Philip to his next assignment many miles away.

8:40 'But Philip found himself at Azotus, and as he passed through he kept preaching the gospel to all the cities until he came to Caesarea.'

Azotus is the Greek name for the ancient Philistine city of Ashdod (1 Samuel 5:21), on the Mediterranean coast. The cities in that region were due for their opportunity to experience the joy of repentance and faith that the Ethiopian had benefited from and Philip's ministry in the office of evangelist continued northwards towards the Roman administrative center of Caesarea, built by Herod the Great in honour of Caesar Augustus, and where Philip himself lived with his family of four daughters (Acts 21:8-9).

Chapter 9

9:1-2 'Now Saul, still breathing threats and murder against the disciples of the Lord, went to the high priest, and asked for letters from him to the synagogues at Damascus, so that if he found any belonging to the Way, both men and women, he might bring them bound to Jerusalem.'

Luke now returns to the direct legal chronology of Saul/Paul, the defendant-to-be in this his second legal treatise written to the Roman lawyer/judge Theophilus for Caesar's court. Saul's mad rage-driven behaviour against all the Jewish followers of the crucified alleged blasphemer Jesus of Nazareth was continuing apace.

Saul had broadened his persecutions to include Jews of the *'diaspora'* -those living 'dispersed' as far away as Damascus, 136 miles to the northeast of Jerusalem in neighbouring Syria. His zeal for orthodox Pharisaic Judaism and his state of extreme agitation and religious outrage towards these distant Jewish followers of Jesus is again evidenced by Luke.

The Greek for 'breathing' threats is *'empneōn'*, the 'rapid gasping' of deeply agitated emotion, in this case, fueling Saul's violent and murderous intentions. As a Sanhedrin associate and Jewish religious lawyer, Saul (soon to be referred to by his Roman name, Paul), had personal access to the High Priest, and was authorized to act as his legally empowered emissary. This is a clear indication of his official standing within the governing body that ruled over Temple Mount, very recently the main place of Jesus' equally legally authorized Judean teaching ministry.

9:3-6 'As he was traveling, it happened that he was approaching Damascus, and suddenly a light from heaven flashed around him; and he fell to the ground and heard a voice saying to him, "Saul, Saul, why are you persecuting me?" And he said, "Who are you, Lord?" And he said, "I am Jesus whom you are persecuting, it is hard for you to kick against the pricks, but get up and enter the city, and it will be told you what you must do."'

Verse 27 makes it clear that it was Jesus himself, in his glorified state, who appeared to Saul in the midst of the bright light. Jesus' human voice would have been known to Saul from Jesus' years of semi-public Temple teaching ministry, but the sudden shock of the heavenly vision throws Saul into confusion, hence his startled question.

Blinded by the powerful light, Paul now gets marching orders from his new master, Jesus the Messiah.

9:7-9 'The men who traveled with him stood speechless, hearing the voice but seeing no one. Saul got up from the ground, and though his eyes were open, he could see nothing; and leading him by the hand, they brought him into Damascus. And he was three days without sight, and neither ate nor drank.'

Whereas Saul loses his sight, his escort loses, temporarily, their power of speech. They can hear Jesus' voice but are not struck blind, the light not being directed at them.

On being led by them into the city Saul, no doubt in a state of profound shock at having been confronted by Jesus in his divinity in such a sudden and unexpected manner, and with the added loss of his sight, withdraws spiritually into a period of prayer and complete fasting, an expression of sorrow for his many sins against God's people.

9:10-16 'Now there was a disciple at Damascus named Ananias; and the Lord said to him in a vision, "Ananias." And he said, "Here I am, Lord." And the Lord said to him, "Get up and go to the street called Straight, and inquire at the house of Judas for a man from Tarsus named Saul, for he is praying, and he has seen in a vision a man named Ananias come in and lay his hands on him, so that he might regain his sight." But Ananias answered, "Lord, I have heard from many about this man, how much harm he did to your saints at Jerusalem; and here he has authority from the chief priests to bind all who call on your name." But the Lord said to him, "Go, for he is a chosen instrument of mine, to bear my name before the Gentiles and kings and the sons of Israel; or I will show him how much he must suffer for my name's sake."

Fortunately the fasting Saul was able to see spiritually if not physically, and is made aware of the prayer ministry of Ananias that is about to come his way. Ananias clearly is accustomed to both seeing and hearing from Jesus, and his high degree of spiritual maturity (see also Acts

22:12) enables him to get past his natural apprehension concerning the danger that Saul's mission posed to him personally. Saul is about to learn of the implications for himself that Jesus' intervention will bring about in his own life; namely, deep personal suffering leading eventually to martyrdom following the ongoing persecution of fellow religious Jews.

9:17-19a 'So Ananias departed and entered the house, and after laying his hands on him said, "Brother Saul, the Lord Jesus, who appeared to you on the road by which you were coming, has sent me so that you may regain your sight and be filled with the Holy Spirit." And immediately there fell from his eyes something like scales, and he regained his sight, and he got up and was baptized; and he took food and was strengthened.'

Ananias gets his perceived to be risky and potentially unpleasant task completed with dispatch, delivering a prayer of faith that resulted in Saul being filled with the Holy Spirit, and his sight is restored as a scaly substance drops away from his eyes. Saul's immediate response is to be baptized, before ending his three day fast.

9:19b-22 'Now for several days he was with the disciples who were at Damascus, and immediately he began to proclaim Jesus in the synagogues, saying, "He is the Son of God." All those hearing him continued to be amazed, and were saying, "Is this not he who in Jerusalem destroyed those who called on this name, and who had come here for the purpose of bringing them bound before the chief priests?" But Saul kept increasing in strength and confounding the Jews who lived at Damascus by proving that this Jesus is the Christ.'

After a few days recuperating with the messianic Jewish fellowship in Damascus Saul is straight into action, deploying his superb grasp of the Old Testament Scriptures combined with his own personal knowledge of Jesus' teaching and ministry from the Temple Courts.

He is easily able to engage in 'proving' Jesus' status as Israel's promised Messiah. The Greek here for proving is *'sumbibazó,* from *'sýn'* - 'to identify with', and *'embibázō'* 'to board a ship'; a word meaning to connect ideas together and so teach them in a joined up message easily comprehensible to one's audience.

9:23-25 'When many days had elapsed, the Jews plotted together to do away with him, but their plot became known to Saul. They were also watching the gates day and night so that they might put him to death; but his disciples took him by night and let him down through an opening in the wall, lowering him in a large basket.'

The religious Jews in Damascus, aware of the Sanhedrin's views on the matter of this new messianic group known as 'The Way', decide that something must be done to stop Saul and enlist the help of the city governor (the *'ethnarch'* - quite possibly a fellow Jew) in facilitating Saul's arrest (1 Corinthians 11:32-33). The disciples have other ideas however, and enable his escape through a window and over the city wall in a basket.

9:26-30 'When he came to Jerusalem, he was trying to associate with the disciples; but they were all afraid of him, not believing that he was a disciple. But Barnabas took hold of him and brought him to the apostles and described to them how he had seen the Lord on the road, and that he had talked to him, and how at Damascus he had spoken out boldly in the name of Jesus. And he was with them, moving about freely in Jerusalem, speaking out boldly in the name of the Lord. And he was talking and arguing with the Hellenistic Jews; but they were attempting to put him to death. But when the brethren learned of it, they brought him down to Caesarea and sent him away to Tarsus. So the church throughout all Judea and Galilee and Samaria enjoyed peace, being built up; and going on in the fear of the Lord and in the comfort of the Holy Spirit, it continued to increase.'

Poor Saul! He went from being threatened in Damascus by his fellow religious Jews to being suspected in Jerusalem of being a Sanhedrin 'plant' sent to spy on the identities of new believers there. Fortunately, the large-hearted Barnabas is on hand to apply a little spiritual discernment, introducing him to the apostles and relating to them the events to date that evidenced the genuineness of Saul's conversion.

Saul's boldly assertive proclamations of Messiah's identity quickly bring him into conflict with his old colleagues at the execution of Stephen. The Hellenists are now planning the same kind of fatal outcome for Saul himself. The believers then take the wise measure of preserving his life by sending him back to his home in Tarsus (south-east modern day Turkey).

Luke then closes the section on Paul's conversion with a description of how peace (*eirênê* -'rest and wholeness'), enabling it to be built up (*oikodomeô* - 'house building') coexisting with both the fear of God and also numerical growth.

The role of the Holy Spirit in this 'comfort' is described as *'paraklésis'* - 'an urging/ exhortation from someone close beside them.' This Spirit led growth in testimony is exactly what Jesus had promised his disciples (John 15:26). Luke's narrative spotlight now moves across to Peter, the main leader in the Jerusalem fellowship at that time.

9:32-35 'Now as Peter was traveling through all those regions, he came down also to the saints who lived at Lydda. There he found a man named Aeneas, who had been bedridden eight years, for he was paralyzed. Peter said to him, "Aeneas, Jesus Christ heals you; get up and make your bed." Immediately he got up. And all who lived at Lydda and Sharon saw him, and they turned to the Lord.'

Lydda was located 10 miles southeast of Joppa on the road from Jerusalem to Caesarea Philippi. The paralysed Aeneas benefits from the experience Jesus' disciples had had with their master in performing similar miraculous healings (Matthew 4:24, Luke 5:24) and the miracle had a profound impact on the surrounding area.

9:36-43 'Now in Joppa there was a disciple named Tabitha (which translated in Greek is called Dorcas); this woman was abounding with deeds of kindness and charity which she continually did. And it happened at that time that she fell sick and died; and when they had washed her body, they laid it in an upper room. Since Lydda was near Joppa, the disciples, having heard that Peter was there, sent two men to him, imploring him, "Do not delay in coming to us." So Peter arose and went with them. When he arrived, they brought him into the upper room; and all the widows stood beside him, weeping and showing all the tunics and garments that Dorcas used to make while she was with them. But Peter sent them all out and knelt down and prayed, and turning to the body, he said, "Tabitha, arise." And she opened her eyes, and when she saw Peter, she sat up. And he gave her his hand and raised her up; and calling the saints and widows, he presented her alive. It became known all over Joppa, and many believed in the Lord. And Peter stayed many days in Joppa with a tanner named Simon.'

Arriving in Joppa (modern Jaffa), the main natural seaport of the region (Chronicles 2:16, Ezra 3:7), Peter is called upon to pray for a local saint, and on arriving, finds that she has died. This doesn't deter Peter, who prays in faith for resurrection. Dorcas (Tabitha) means 'graceful doe' and this woman was undoubtedly grace-filled, in life, death and then in life once again.

Peter then demonstrates his non-compliance with the prevailing legalistic mindsets of the mainstream religious Jews by staying with a tanner, a man legally unclean by reason of his occupation bringing him into contact with the skins of dead animals.

Leviticus (11:8) required washing of clothing and the wearer was deemed unclean until the evening. Jesus' foremost disciple was clearly not abiding by the strict applications of the Jew's purification laws.

Chapter 10

10:1-8 'Now there was a man at Caesarea named Cornelius, a centurion of what was called the Italian cohort, a devout man and one who feared God with all his household, and gave many alms to the Jewish people and prayed to God continually. About the ninth hour of the day he clearly saw in a vision an angel of God who had just come in and said to him, "Cornelius!" And fixing his gaze on him and being much alarmed, he said, "What is it, Lord?" And he said to him, "Your prayers and alms have ascended as a memorial before God. "Now dispatch some men to Joppa and send for a man named Simon, who is also called Peter; he is staying with a tanner named Simon, whose house is by the sea." When the angel who was speaking to him had left, he summoned two of his servants and a devout soldier of those who were his personal attendants, and after he had explained everything to them, he sent them to Joppa.'

A Roman army cohort consisted of 600 men, within which the centurion Cornelius was responsible for the command of 100 soldiers. He was a devout 'God-fearer', who prayed 'continually' The Greek word here is *'dia'*, also meaning 'thoroughly', and while praying at the (Jewish) hour of evening prayer (3pm), he receives the angelic messenger with *'emphobos'* ('fearfulness', rather than 'alarm'), but with a 'steadiness' of gaze indicative of one used to receiving orders while in apparent adversity.

The 'memorial' of Cornelius' prayer offerings towards God is 'mnémosunon' - a 'remembrance offering' before the God of Israel, who is about to send Cornelius into history as the first God fearer Gentile to be filled with the Holy Spirit.

The passage is the point at which Luke's underlying legal agenda starts in earnest. Namely, to show that the new Messianic Jewish faith now part of Judaism was no threat to Rome. He would also show that Paul was a good Roman citizen who had not offended against Rome's laws at all. Just as in his first (Gospel) treatise, Luke details a very Roman-friendly account of the new messianic faith's beginnings. Luke highlights its many positive features and presents Paul in a light that Caesar's court in Rome could have found no possible legal or moral fault with.

What was good enough for the famous Italian military cohort would one day prove to be good enough for Caesar's Court in Rome.

10:9-16 'On the next day, as they were on their way and approaching the city, Peter went up on the housetop about the sixth hour to pray. But he became hungry and was desiring to eat; but while they were making preparations, he fell into a trance; and he saw the sky opened up, and an object like a great sheet coming down, lowered by four corners to the ground, and there were in it all kinds of four-footed animals and crawling creatures of the earth and birds of the air. A voice came to him, "Get up, Peter, kill and eat!" But Peter said, "By no means, Lord, for I have never eaten anything unholy and unclean." Again a voice came to him a second time, "What God has cleansed, no longer consider unholy."

This happened three times, and immediately the object was taken up into the sky.'

Meanwhile, back in Joppa, Peter's prayer time is making him rather hungry, and he falls into 'a trance'. The Greek here is *'ekstasis'*, meaning an ecstatic 'bewilderment of the mind'.

The vision of legally unclean animals is representative of the approaching Gentiles rather than a re-writing of God given (Levitical) food laws. Peter was able to profess Jewish purity whilst staying in the house of a tanner, evidence of his progression from the Law under Jesus' personal spiritual tutelage.

10:17-23 'Now while Peter was greatly perplexed in mind as to what the vision which he had seen might be, behold, the men who had been sent by Cornelius, having asked directions for Simon's house, appeared at the gate; and calling out, they were asking whether Simon, who was also called Peter, was staying there. While Peter was reflecting on the vision, the Spirit said to him, "Behold, three men are looking for you. "But get up, go downstairs and accompany them without misgivings, for I have sent them myself." Peter went down to the men and said, "Behold, I am the one you are looking for; what is the reason for which you have come?" They said, "Cornelius, a centurion, a righteous and God-fearing man well spoken of by the entire nation of the Jews, was divinely directed by a holy angel to send for you to come to his house and hear a message from you." So he invited them in and gave them lodging.'

'Perplexed in mind' here is *'dieporei'*, also meaning 'nonplussed'. This leads to further prayerful 'reflection' and 'pondering' on Peter's part. Peter's 'reflecting' is *'dienthymoumenoun'*, meaning to 'meditate upon' (prayerfully, in this case) from *'enthyme'* - to 'fervently cogitate'.

The impact of the incongruous heavenly vision upon Peter was therefore to drive him even deeper into prayer so as to ask God for its meaning, and in direct consequence he was able to be sufficiently in-tune with the Holy Spirit to be able to go with the Cornelius' servants without having all the immediate answers but with an active willingness to let God do whatever further guiding was needful.

10:24-29: 'And on the next day he got up and went away with them, and some of the brethren from Joppa accompanied him. On the following day he entered Caesarea. Now Cornelius was waiting for them and had called together his relatives and close friends. When Peter entered, Cornelius met him, and fell at his feet and worshiped him. But Peter raised him up, saying, "Stand up; I too am just a man." As he talked with him, he entered and found many people assembled. And he said to them, "You yourselves know how unlawful it is for a man who is a Jew to associate with a foreigner or to visit him; and yet God has shown me that I should not call any man unholy or unclean. "That is why I came without even raising any objection when I was sent for. So I ask for what reason you have sent for me."'

Going anywhere with members of the occupying Roman army represented rising to God's challenge on Peter's part, and especially into the Roman/Gentile center of civic administration that was Caesarea Philippi. This had been established at the southwest base of Mount Hermon by Alexander the Great (who had named it 'Paneas' after the Greek god Pan, and it was later annexed for Rome by Herod the Great (who built a large white temple there in honour of Caesar).

Caesarea Philippi became the headquarters of Philip II, (son of Herod the Great and his fifth wife, Cleopatra of Jerusalem), who was allotted the northeast section of his father's kingdom by the emperor Augustus.

It was Philip II who notoriously married Salome, daughter of Princess Herodias and Herod II (the son of Herod the Great and his third wife, Mariamne II). This, of course, was much to the disquiet of John the Baptist (see Matthew 14:3-5).

Cornelius shows no inhibitions in expressing towards Peter what was, to him, due recognition of the role God had for Peter to play in Cornelius' life. 'Worship' here is *'prosekynesen'*, meaning a reverent posture of prostration, rather than some misguided view of divinity.

Peter, probably recalling his initial outraged reaction to the vision he had received on Simon the Tanner's rooftop, quickly disabuses him of the need for such an exceedingly respectful response.

The Talmud (*Sanhedrin* 56 a-b) forbade entry for devout Jews into (pagan) Gentile dwellings, as a ring-fence measure against the negative influence of what it refers to as *'oved kokhavim u-mazzalot'* – the 'worshippers of stars and planets'.

These were 'idolaters' of whom the occupying Romans were very definitely numbered amongst by observant Jews.

Peter seems to have digested and absorbed the lesson of the heavenly vision and puts these cultural and religious-legal issues to one side in order to follow the revealed will of God.

10:30-33 'Cornelius said, "Four days ago to this hour, I was praying in my house during the ninth hour; and behold, a man stood before me in shining garments, and he said, 'Cornelius, your prayer has been heard and your alms have been remembered before God. 'Therefore send to Joppa and invite Simon, who is also called Peter, to come to you; he is staying at the house of Simon the tanner by the sea.' So I sent for you immediately, and you have been kind enough to come. Now then, we are all here present before God to hear all that you have been commanded by the Lord."'

Cornelius' faith is such that he knows that Peter will have been 'commanded', just as he, an elite Roman soldier, is accustomed to regularly receiving orders and directions.

The term used is *'prostetagmena'* - 'to instruct and assign.' God had assigned his servant Peter to serve his word to this senior Roman soldier. Cornelius repeats the angel's comments concerning the favour with which his prayers and charitable deeds ('*eleemosune*' - acts of mercy, most commonly financial giving/alms) had been received before the throne of Almighty God in heaven.

He and his God-fearing Roman household now waited, in faith, to hear Peter's message.

10:34-43 'Opening his mouth, Peter said: "I most certainly understand now that God is not one to show partiality, but in every nation the man who fears him and does what is right is welcome to him. The word which he sent to the sons of Israel, preaching peace through Jesus Christ - (he is Lord of all) - you yourselves know the thing which took place throughout all Judea, starting from Galilee, after the baptism which John proclaimed. You know of Jesus of Nazareth, how God anointed him with the Holy Spirit and with power, and how he went about doing good and healing all who were oppressed by the devil, for God was with him. We are witnesses of all the things he did both in the land of the Jews and in Jerusalem. They also put him to death by hanging him on a cross. God raised him up on the third day and granted that e become visible, not to all the people, but to witnesses who were chosen beforehand by God, that is, to us who ate and drank with him after he arose from the dead. And he ordered us to preach to the people, and solemnly to testify that this is the One who has been appointed by God as Judge of the living and the dead. Of him all the prophets bear witness that through his name everyone who believes in him receives forgiveness of sins."

Peter was from a faith and culture that historically very strongly believed that Almighty God favoured his people Israel. He now understands that God's favour, perfectly expressed in Jesus' substitutionary sacrifice, extends far beyond simply those within God's covenant with Abraham. 'Partiality' is *'prosōpolēmptēs'* - from *'prosopon'* and *'lambano'*; meaning an 'accepter of a face', such that a degree of favouritism and positive prejudice is exercised. There are many 'foreign' people groups in the world today whose hearts and lifestyles are significantly more inclined towards God than many in the increasingly apostate, but traditionally 'Christian' West.

Very significantly Peter takes it for granted ("You know of Jesus") that this Roman household in Caesarea Philippi is already familiar with the societal identity and the human back-story of Jesus, which was undoubtedly linked to the identity and role of his earthly father Joseph within the ruling Roman society of that day.

The fact that Peter does so reinforces the perspective described by John (John 6:42), where the Jewish public in the Galilean Roman capital of Capernaum say, "Is this not Jesus, whose father and mother **we know**?" Jesus' family were therefore well known in Roman circles, surely due to the senior role that the specialist *'tekton'* (architect-builder/structural engineer) Joseph played in overseeing the major Roman sponsored construction works. These would have included the Temple of Herod as well as the defensive fortifications at Sepphoris, six kilometers to the northwest of Nazareth.

Additionally, Jesus' teaching and miracles had led to him becoming a regional household name in his own right. Peter delivers his eyewitness testimony concerning Jesus' crucifixion and resurrection, along with Jesus' parting commands regarding proclaiming the truth of it with personal testimony as to its saving power.

10:44-48 'While Peter was still speaking these words, the Holy Spirit fell upon all those who were listening to the message. All the circumcised believers who came with Peter were amazed, because the gift of the Holy Spirit had been poured out on the Gentiles also. For they were hearing them speaking with tongues and exalting God. Then Peter answered, "Surely no one can refuse the water for these to be baptized who have received the Holy Spirit just as we did, can he?" And he ordered them to be baptized in the name of Jesus Christ. Then they asked him to stay on for a few days.'

God now endorses Peter's message of salvation with an outpouring of his Holy Spirit, to the astonishment of the Jewish believers accompanying Peter.

God was definitely not favouring the Jews only, and having himself been commanded by God to cross major racial and cultural lines, Peter now commands that water be provided for baptism, thus making history by formally including Gentiles within the New Covenant for the first time.

Chapter 11

11:1-3 'Now the apostles and the brethren who were throughout Judea heard that the Gentiles also had received the word of God. And when Peter came up to Jerusalem, those who were circumcised took issue with him, saying, "You went to uncircumcised men and ate with them.

The shocking nature of God's intervention with the Gentiles was more than sufficient to trigger an enquiry by the rest of the Apostles back in Jerusalem. Therefore Peter fully recounts the episode, expounding and explaining what he had done in consequence of the thrice demonstrated revelation that God had cleansed that which was previously considered unclean, namely the Gentile God-fearers. Eating and even entering the house of a Gentile was forbidden by the Rabbinic Oral Law ('*Shulchan Aruch Yoreh Deah*' 152), itself based upon Exodus 34:15, which warns against eating of idolater's sacrifices.

11:4-11 'But Peter began speaking and proceeded to explain to them in orderly sequence, saying, "I was in the city of Joppa praying; and in a trance I saw a vision, an object coming down like a great sheet lowered by four corners from the sky; and it came right down to me, and when I had fixed my gaze on it and was observing it I saw the four-footed animals of the earth and the wild beasts and the crawling creatures and the birds of the air. "I also heard a voice saying to me, 'Get up, Peter; kill and eat.' But I said, 'By no means, Lord, for nothing unholy or unclean has ever entered my mouth.' But a voice from heaven answered a second time, 'What God has cleansed, no longer consider unholy.' This happened three times, and everything was drawn back up into the sky. And behold, at that moment three men appeared at the house in which we were staying, having been sent to me from Caesarea."

The 'object' Peter refers to is *'skeous',* meaning 'vessel', the clay pots very commonly used for storage. The 'wild beasts and crawling creatures' described are clearly unlawful for Jews to eat, hence Peter's startled response to God's command that he should kill and eat them. Fortunately God expanded upon this in commanding Peter not to consider as unholy that which God has defined as cleansed (*'katharizo'* - 'purified').

Peter interpreted this as indicating that it was lawful to accept the invitation to accompany Cornelius' servants and to eat with them. He did not thereafter cease observing the Levitical food laws commanded to Moses by God. Jesus had taught (Matthew 15:11, Mark 7:18-19) that it was what came from the heart via the mouth that rendered a person 'unclean', not food that went into the mouth to be simply expelled from the bowel in human waste.

Some translations of Mark's account add a note in parentheses that states that Jesus was declaring all foods to be 'clean' in a Judaistic legal sense. The Codex Sinaiticus does not include this statement which would be a direct contradiction of Jesus' own commands as the giver of the law to Moses in Exodus and Leviticus.

Peter's reaction to being told to eat from the lowered vessel from heaven clearly illustrates this. If Jesus had in fact declared 'all foods' to be clean then Peter would clearly not have reacted in this manner.

11:12-18 "The Spirit told me to go with them without misgivings. These six brethren also went with me and we entered the man's house. And he reported to us how he had seen the angel standing in his house, and saying, 'Send to Joppa and have Simon, who is also called Peter, brought here; and he will speak words to you by which you will be saved, you and all your household.' And I remembered the word of the Lord, how he used to say, 'John baptized with water, but you will be baptized with the Holy Spirit.' Therefore if God gave to them the same gift as he gave to us also after believing in the Lord Jesus Christ, who was I that I could stand in God's way?" When they heard this, they quieted down and glorified God, saying, "Well then, God has granted to the Gentiles also the repentance that leads to life."'

Peter's firsthand experience of the events in the upper room when the promised baptism with the Holy Spirit arrived now undergirds his explanation of this 'Gentile Pentecost'. The other disciples of Messiah then *'hésuchazó'*, experiencing the inner 'tranquility' that God gives when the believer recognizes God's sovereignty and submits to it, despite their own personal prejudices and preconceived ideas.

11:19-21 'So then those who were scattered because of the persecution that occurred in connection with Stephen made their way to Phoenicia and Cyprus and Antioch, speaking the word to no one except to Jews alone. But there were some of them, men of Cyprus and Cyrene, who came to Antioch and began speaking to the Greeks also, preaching the Lord Jesus. And the hand of the Lord was with them, and a large number who believed turned to the Lord.

God's plan to disseminate the seed of his good news of Messiah's sacrifice turned the persecution of the infant church to positive effect. Initially the message went just to the 'lost sheep of the house of Israel', but soon the Jewish believers with Greek as their first language began to share the gospel with fellow non-Jewish Greek speakers. This was clearly under the inspiration of the Holy Spirit, as evidenced by the very good fruit borne.

11:22-24 'The news about them reached the ears of the church at Jerusalem, and they sent Barnabas off to Antioch. Then when he arrived and witnessed the grace of God, he rejoiced and began to encourage them all with resolute heart to remain true to the Lord; for he was a good man, and full of the Holy Spirit and of faith. And considerable numbers were brought to the Lord.'

Enter once again the Cypriot Jew (the son of Joseph, a Levite) known as the 'son of encouragement'. The name Barnabas is likely derived from the Aramaic *'bar naviya'*, meaning the 'son of the prophet', and re-rendered by the Apostles as the 'son of encouragement' (Acts 4:16).

True to his name he *'parakaleós'* - the new believers in Antioch - 'encouraging' them to continue and remain faithful to the Lord.

11:25-30 'And he left for Tarsus to look for Saul; and when he had found him, he brought him to Antioch. And for an entire year they met with the church and taught considerable numbers; and the disciples were first called Christians in Antioch. Now at this time some prophets came down from Jerusalem to Antioch. One of them named Agabus stood up and began to indicate by the Spirit that there would certainly be a great famine all over the world. And this took place in the reign of Claudius. And in the proportion that any of the disciples had means, each of them determined to send *a* contribution for the relief of the brethren living in Judea. And this they did, sending it in charge of Barnabas and Saul to the elders.'

Understanding that the infant gentile church required more than his own gifts were able to supply, Barnabas departs for Saul's hometown of Tarsus in Roman Cilicia (modern south-eastern Turkey) to get help from one of the best Scripture experts available.

Saul had been fully occupied both in coming to terms with the shock of both meeting Jesus and also realizing that he'd been misguidedly murdering godly Jews. He was persuaded to respond to the need to teach these Gentile converts about the Hebrew Scriptures that undergirded their newfound faith in the Jewish Messiah.

So serious was their desire for a secure biblical foundation that the fellowship devoted a full year to receiving Saul's teaching input. No doubt this was based on both Saul's Hebrew Scriptural expertise and also upon his repeated exposure to Jesus' recent Temple teaching ministry.

Such was the efficacy of Saul's ministry that the believers were transforming into mini versions of Jesus, and were therefore referred to publicly as *'Christianos'*, literally meaning 'Christ's ones'. This term was used by non believers initially in a derogatory manner, and continued to be so for many decades; with Tacitus recording that 'the vulgar call them Christians'. The early believers actually chose to refer to themselves as 'followers of the Way' (Acts 9:2).

The early disciples focused outwardly as well as inwardly. When the prophetic indication of coming hardship and famine was heard (and doubtless also tested spiritually), they responded with a generosity characteristic of a genuine move of the Holy Spirit.

Claudius Caesar began his reign in 41 A.D. and reigned for 13 years before being poisoned by one of his wives, Agrippina, who wished to see her son Nero reach the throne. During Claudius' reign a number of different famines occurred, one of which was particularly severe in Judea.

This particular one is described by Josephus as follows:
'A famine oppressed them at the time of Claudius and many people died for the lack of what was necessary to procure food for all. Queen Helena sent some of her servants to Alexandria with money to buy a great quantity of grain, and others of them to Cyprus to bring a cargo of dried figs.' ('Antiquities', 20, 2,5)

This famine is described as having continued under the two procurators of Judea, Tiberius Alexander and Cassius Fadus. Fadus was sent into Judea, on the death of Agrippa, about the fourth year of the reign of Claudius, and the famine is believed to have continued during the fifth, sixth, and seventh years of the reign of Claudius.

Saul did not restrict himself to simply exercising his considerable gift of teaching, but also accompanied Barnabas on the church's charitable mission, thereby underlining his commitment to serving those in need materially as well as spiritually.

James the brother of John had assured Jesus that they were both capable of drinking from Jesus' cup of suffering. While John most assuredly suffered greatly in his service of Messiah, it was James who paid the ultimate price first.

Chapter 12

12:1-5 'Now about that time Herod the king laid hands on some who belonged to the church in order to mistreat them. And he had James the brother of John put to death with a sword. When he saw that it pleased the Jews, he proceeded to arrest Peter also. Now it was during the days of Unleavened Bread. When he had seized him, he put him in prison, delivering him to four squads of soldiers to guard him, intending after the Passover to bring him out before the people. So Peter was kept in the prison, but prayer for him was being made fervently by the church to God.'

Once again Luke writes with a Roman-trial friendly hand. At the time of writing, around 63 AD, this particular Herod (Herod Agrippa I) had a questionable and highly chequered track record with Rome. Agrippa was Herod the Great's grandson via Aristobulus and nephew of Herod Antipas. He had been sent to Rome for his education by Herod the Great (after he had had Agrippa's father Aristobulus strangled in 7BC), where Agrippa had been warmly received by Emperor Tiberius and had grown up in Rome as a close friend of the young Caligula.

His later support of Caligula to become emperor over the head of Tiberius' own son Drusus incurred him the displeasure of Tiberius, who had Agrippa imprisoned, suspecting him of plotting to usurp his authority. Agrippa had also run up many personal debts, funding a very extravagant personal lifestyle.

His uncle, Herod Antipas, had to befriend him with gifts of money even though Agrippa held a paid administrative role in Antipas' district of Tiberias. The headstrong Agrippa quarreled with Antipas over money and he fled to Syria, where he fell under suspicion of plotting with Damascus against Roman rule.

Agrippa was eventually arrested for his unpaid debts but managed to escape custody, fleeing to Alexandria in Egypt, where he was befriended by Philo's brother Alexander. Eventually returning to Rome he was received there (initially) favourably by Emperor Tiberius and was able to renew his friendship with Caligula. It was then that Tiberius imprisoned Agrippa on suspicion of treason. When Caligula finally succeeded from Tiberius he presented Agrippa with a gold chain equal in weight to the iron chain that Tiberius had bound him with in prison.

Agrippa later dedicated this immensely valuable gold chain to the Temple in Jerusalem, further earning him the favour of its Sanhedrin priestly rulers.

In 39AD Agrippa informed Rome about Herod Antipas' treasonable military aspirations, helping to bring about Antipas' banishment to Gaul. Caligula rewarded Agrippa with his late uncle Philip the Tetrarch's territories of Galilee and Peraea. Agrippa now almost matched his grandfather Herod the Great in terms of territorial rule over the region surrounding Israel, and would soon surpass him.

When Claudius succeeded to the role of Emperor following Caligula's assassination in 41AD, he further rewarded Agrippa with rulership over Judea and Samaria.

Now a hugely powerful Roman-Judean ruler, Agrippa heavily fortified Jerusalem, an act that incurred the newly ruling Claudius' displeasure amid suspicions of further treasonable ambitions.

Agrippa was, however, very popular with the Judean local rulers (he had from an early age been 'pleasing the Jews' - verse 2). He had been very instrumental in blocking Caligula in his wish to set up his image in statue form in the Temple in 41AD, something that would have triggered great civil unrest within Israel.

By the time Paul's trial had occurred, Nero's Court would have certainly recalled Agrippa's long record of poor behaviour and understand just how malign an influence upon the early believers he must have been.

The shock of losing James combined with Peter's arrest drove the Judean disciples to their knees - 'fervent' prayer is *'ekteno'*- 'earnestly resolute'. Agrippa was in no hurry to kill Peter, but was instead looking forward to a public show trial once the busy Passover festival was over.

He may have been anticipating resistance from the now large numbers of believing Jews dwelling in Jerusalem. 'Four squads' of soldiers (*'tetradion'*) totals 16 men, a very large number to guard just one man given the considerable strength of Antonia as a major Roman fortress.

12:6-8 'On the very night when Herod was about to bring him forward, Peter was sleeping between two soldiers, bound with two chains, and guards in front of the door were watching over the prison. And behold, an angel of the Lord suddenly appeared and a light shone in the cell; and he struck Peter's side and woke him up, saying, ``Get up quickly." And his chains fell off his hands. And the angel said to him, "Gird yourself and put on your sandals." And he did so. And he said to him, "Wrap your cloak around you and follow me."'

As Peter experienced, God's tests of faith frequently continue until the very last possible moment, when any hope of a human answer has been diminished greatly.

Agrippa's maximum security measures would not interfere with the overriding plans of the One who had created the very raw materials that gave Agrippa the illusion of control. All his chains and Roman military guards were no match for a single angel.

Without delay, the angel strikes Peter into wakefulness, facilitating his responsiveness by miraculously removing his chains. The desire for haste didn't prevent angelic concern for human core temperature. The cloak in first century Jewish life doubled as a necessary blanket at night and cells in the fortress of Antonia were certainly not heated.

12:9-10 'And he went out and continued to follow, and he did not know that what was being done by the angel was real, but thought he was seeing a vision. When they had passed the first and second guard, they came to the iron gate that leads into the city, which opened for them by itself; and they went out and went along one street, and immediately the angel departed from him.'

Still sleepy and unsure if he was dreaming, Peter became aware that it was actually Herod Agrippa's men who were sleeping. In a God induced coma, these men would have no recollection of the events, and be unable to give any account of the night's escape. Even the prison gates silently cooperate. Once the angel is satisfied that his mission has been accomplished, Peter is left to his own devices.

12:11-12 'When Peter came to himself, he said, "Now I know for sure that the Lord has sent forth his angel and rescued me from the hand of Herod and from all that the Jewish people were expecting." And when he realized this, he went to the house of Mary, the mother of John who was also called Mark, where many were gathered together and were praying.'

Lucidity restored, Peter heads for the Jerusalem congregation meeting in Mark's mother Mary's house, where a prayer meeting for his release was in progress. Happily, the object of those prayers was about to knock on Mary's door.

12:13-15 'When he knocked at the door of the gate, a servant-girl named Rhoda came to answer. When she recognized Peter's voice, because of her joy she did not open the gate, but ran in and announced that Peter was standing in front of the gate. They said to her, "You are out of your mind!" But she kept insisting that it was so. They kept saying, "It is his angel."'

Poor Rhoda, and poor unbelieving church! Jesus had posed the rhetorical question of Peter, "When he son of man comes, will he find faith?" (Luke 18:8). Peter, himself finding none, is kept waiting outside, just as modern unbelief frequently also excludes Jesus, despite religious appearances.

12:16-17 'But Peter continued knocking; and when they had opened the door, they saw him and were amazed. But motioning to them with his hand to be silent, he described to them how the Lord had led him out of the prison. And he said, "Report these things to James and the brethren." Then he left and went to another place.'

Eventually Peter's persistence and Rhoda's insistence won through and those praying became amazed that God had in fact already answered them. Peter left a brief message for James the half-brother of Jesus, who had great reputational standing in Jerusalem and who had been appointed to church leadership after coming to personal faith following Jesus' resurrection.

12:18-19 'Now when day came, there was no small disturbance among the soldiers as to what could have become of Peter. When Herod had searched for him and had not found him, he examined the guards and ordered that they be led away to execution. Then he went down from Judea to Caesarea and was spending time there.'

Meanwhile consternation and confusion reign in the imposing fortress of Antonia. Agrippa has no hesitation in summarily executing the night shift prior to leaving for Rome's regional headquarters to the north at Caesarea Philippi.

12:20-22 'Now he was very angry with the people of Tyre and Sidon; and with one accord they came to him, and having won over Blastus the king's chamberlain, they were asking for peace, because their country was fed by the king's country. On an appointed day Herod, having put on his royal apparel, took his seat on the rostrum and began delivering an address to them. The people kept crying out, "The voice of a god and not of a man!"'

Food supplies were a constant worry in the ancient world. Tyre and Sidon were coastal regions notorious for recently having become home to sea going pirates that stole grain exports bound for Rome. Their residents were now experiencing a taste of their own medicine.

Luke knows these details will resonate with his Roman legal audience, who would well recall the recent pirate-driven scarcity of bread in their empire's capital that had led to much social unrest in Rome.

Josephus' account also specifically mentions Agrippa's royal robes, which were made from a very expensive silver cloth. This reflected the sun's rays, prompting the mostly Gentile crowd to liken him to a god. This occurred some years following Augustus' proclamation as Emperor of divinity, however, successive Roman rulers had yet to extend this privilege to client-king debtors and former jailbirds such as Agrippa.

Agrippa had had John's brother and Jesus' cousin James executed, and having failed to add Peter's death to that non-achievement, had gone to Caesarea to open the Roman games there on behalf of the Emperor Caligula.

Josephus records:

'Agrippa exhibited shows in honour of Caesar, upon his being informed that there was a certain festival celebrated to make vows for his [Caesar's] safety. At which festival a great multitude was gathered together of the principal persons, and such as was of dignity through his province. On the second day of which shows he put on a garment made wholly of silver[thread], and of a contexture truly wonderful, and came into the theater early in the morning; at which time the silver of his garment being illuminated by the fresh reflection of the sun's rays upon it, shone out after a surprising manner, and was so resplendent as to spread a horror over those that looked intently upon him; and presently his flatterers cried out, one from one place, and another from another, (though not for his good,) that he was a god; and they added, "Be thou merciful to us; for although we have hitherto reverenced thee only as a man, yet shall we henceforth own thee as superior to mortal nature." Upon this the king did neither rebuke them, nor reject their impious flattery.

But as he presently afterward looked up, he saw an owl sitting on a certain rope over his head, and immediately understood that this bird was the messenger of ill tidings, as it had once been the messenger of good tidings to him; and fell into the deepest sorrow. A severe pain also arose in his belly, and began in a most violent manner. He therefore looked upon his friends, and said, "I, whom you call a god, am commanded presently to depart this life; while Providence thus reproves the lying words you just now said to me; and I, who was by you called immortal, am immediately to be hurried away by death. His **pain became violent**. Accordingly he was carried into the palace, and the rumour went abroad everywhere, that he would certainly die.'

12:23 'And immediately an angel of the Lord struck him because, he did not give God the glory, and he was eaten by worms and died.'

Josephus' account continues:
'And when he had been quite worn out by the pain in his belly for five days, he departed this life, being in the fifty-fourth year of his age, and in the seventh year of his reign; for he reigned four years under Caius Caesar, three of them were over Philip's tetrarchy only, and on the fourth he had that of Herod added to it; and he reigned, besides those, three years under the reign of Claudius Caesar; in which time he reigned over the fore

mentioned countries, and also had Judea added to them, as well as Samaria and Caesarea. The revenues that he received out of them were very great, no less than twelve millions of drachmae. Yet did he borrow great sums from others; for he was so very liberal that his expenses exceeded his income.' ('Antiquities', 8, 11, 22-23 and 19,8,2).

Luke the physician confirms Josephus' historical record, with the additional medical detail that Agrippa's sudden abdominal pain was caused by a worm infestation, this being a very common malady in the days before meat refrigeration.

12:24-25 'But the word of the Lord continued to grow and to be multiplied. And Barnabas and Saul returned from Jerusalem when they had fulfilled their mission, taking along with them John, who was also called Mark.'

Unlike Agrippa, God's word had and still has no need to pretend to be anything other than the source of spiritual life. Like any good seed it has power within itself to reproduce and spread under the oversight of the Holy Spirit who first breathed it into being.

What God is still seeking are believers with the priceless gifts of awareness and availability in his service. Barnabas and Saul had responded to the Judean's needs from Antioch and they now needed assistance in continuing the work of disseminating the good news of Messiah's sacrifice among the Gentile God-fearers.

Mary's son John Mark, the young cousin of Barnabas, was one such person available and willing to assist.

Chapter 13

13:1-3 'Now there were at Antioch, in the church that was there, prophets and teachers: Barnabas, and Simeon who was called Niger, and Lucius of Cyrene, and Manaen who had been brought up with Herod the tetrarch, and Saul. While they were ministering to the Lord and fasting, the Holy Spirit said, "Set apart for me Barnabas and Saul for the work to which I have called them." Then, when they had fasted and prayed and laid their hands on them, they sent them away.'

Having given in his Gospel the exact circumstances of how this messianic offshoot of Judaism had arisen, Luke now begins to focus on the specific case history of Theophilus' new client, Saul/Paul of Tarsus, who had encountered Messiah in such a public and dramatic manner. Antioch contained a thriving mixed assembly of Jewish and Gentile followers of the Way.

There was also a mixture of ministry calling and gift in the 'church.' The term used is *'ekklêsia'* - the same word used by Greeks to denote groups of civilian leaders assembling for the purpose of civic government. This new form of assembly constituted the spiritual leaders of God's governance on earth.

The ministry of the prophet was at the forefront of the early Jewish believers' spiritual life. Based upon centuries of Hebrew practice, prophets were those men and women sufficiently in tune with the Holy Spirit to be able to impart the input that God wished to give. The potential for misuse is enormous, as a future religions emerged to demonstrate. Clear Scriptural teaching and godly oversight is vital, a necessity later born out in Paul's first pastoral letter to the equally mixed race port-city church at Corinth.

Many of the new Gentile converts lacked the grounding in the Hebrew Scriptures taken for granted by the Jewish believers, so teaching was an equally vital part of the ministry equation. After miraculous signs, Jesus main reputation was as a Torah trained *'didaskalôs'*. With the outpouring of the Spirit, this source of spiritual truth became very widely distributed, enabling many others to emulate Jesus' teaching ministry.

Luke has already introduced Barnabas (a Jewish Cypriot). Simeon is a Jewish name while 'Niger' (meaning 'black') indicates Roman-African origin. While the text doesn't indicate his exact place of origin, he at least shares his name with the (Libyan) Simon of Cyrene who was forced to assist Jesus in carrying his cross (Luke 23:26).

Manaen was a Jewish nobleman who had been sent to Rome to be educated there along with others from the ruling Herodian family, whereas Saul/Paul was a highly Torah trained Pharisee from the important Roman city of Tarsus in Cilicia in Southern Turkey.

These four men appear to have been the main leaders in the church at Antioch.

From them the Holy Spirit indicated that Paul and Barnabas had been selected for a specific task, one that would become known as Paul's first missionary journey.

13:4-5 'So, being sent out by the Holy Spirit, they went down to Seleucia and from there they sailed to Cyprus. When they reached Salamis, they began to proclaim the word of God in the synagogues of the Jews; and they also had John as their helper.'

Seleucia was Antioch's port city, with good connections to Cyprus' Salamis. Barnabas would have been at home there as would his cousin John Mark.

13:6-7 'When they had gone through the whole island as far as Paphos, they found a magician, a Jewish false prophet whose name was Bar-Jesus, who was with the proconsul, Sergius Paulus, a man of intelligence. This man summoned Barnabas and Saul and sought to hear the word of God.'

Led by the Holy Spirit, the apostolic team encounters some local spiritual opposition. Bar-Jesus was a *'pseudoprophêtê* s' - a false bringer of spiritual truth who served as an advisor to the local Roman ruler, whom Luke describes as *'sunetos'*,- 'intelligent', and also meaning 'perceptive' and 'sagacious'. When the counterfeit encountered the reality, Bar-Jesus found himself exposed to a spiritual light that clearly revealed his false spirituality.

13:8-12 'But Elymas the magician (for so his name is translated) was opposing them, seeking to turn the proconsul away from the faith. But Saul, who was also known as Paul, filled with the Holy Spirit, fixed his gaze on him, and said, "You who are full of all deceit and fraud, you son of the devil, you enemy of all righteousness, will you not cease to make crooked the straight ways of the Lord? Now, behold, the hand of the Lord is upon you, and you will be blind and not see the sun for a time." And immediately a mist and darkness fell upon him, and he went about seeking those who would lead him by the hand. Then the proconsul believed when he saw what had happened, being amazed at the teaching of the Lord.'

'Elymas' is a Hebrew name, meaning 'wise'. Seeing his deceptive influence over the governor weakening, Bar-Jesus becomes more vocal in opposition whereupon Saul's Spirit-filled and legally trained mind exercises right judgment, backed up by God himself. The Roman proconsul, struck by a remarkable miracle, finds himself receiving the equally miraculous gift of faith in God and the Messiah. Luke is well aware that the Imperial powers that ruled in Rome would likely have heard from Sergius about these events and would have welcomed them.

13:13-15 'Now Paul and his companions, put out to sea from Paphos and came to Perga in Pamphylia; but John left them and returned to Jerusalem. But going on from Perga, they arrived at Pisidian Antioch, and on the Sabbath day they went into the synagogue and sat down. After the reading of the Law and the Prophets the synagogue officials sent to them, saying, "Brethren, if you have any word of exhortation for the people, say it."'

Mission accomplished, the next stop is Perga, on the river Cestris, 12 miles Northeast of Attalia (Antalya in modern day Turkey). Here their young helper John Mark returned to his family home in Israel. His decision to leave the mission did not sit well with Paul (see Acts 15:38). Paul and Barnabas pressed on without him up the dangerous hill road towards Pisidian Antioch.

The largely Jewish early evangelists continued Jesus' ministry of taking the good news of the gospel first to their fellow Jews, hence the visit to the local synagogue. Paul was well recognised as a learned Pharisee from the Jerusalem Temple's Torah school of Rabbi Gamaliel, and so he is invited to speak to the Jewish congregation.

13:16-19 'Paul stood up, and motioning with his hand said,

"Men of Israel, and you who fear God, listen: The God of this people Israel chose our fathers and made the people great during their stay in the land of Egypt, and with an uplifted arm he led them out from it. For a period of about forty years he put up with them in the wilderness. When he had destroyed seven nations in the land of Canaan, he distributed their land as an inheritance - all of which took about four hundred and fifty years."'

Rabbis preceded authoritative teaching with a particular hand gesture, calling for an inner quietness from which to receive God's words. Paul begins his address by reminding his Jewish audience of their deliverance from

Egypt, in a manner reminiscent of the Passover Seder service.

13:20-22 'After these things he gave them judges until Samuel the prophet. Then they asked for a king, and God gave them Saul the son of Kish, a man of the tribe of Benjamin, for forty years. After he had removed him, he raised up David to be their king, concerning whom he also testified and said, `I have found David the son of Jesse, a man after my own heart, who will do all my will."

The salvation history theme continues with the coning of the kings of Israel, commencing with Paul's namesake Saul and the young future King David.

'Heart' in a Hebrew context has a number of different meanings. When God describes David as being 'after his own heart' (1 Samuel 13:14), God is saying that David's central driving intention was to follow God's ways. This is clearly evident in David's worshipful disposition, one nurtured by his musical and lyrical aptitude while shepherding his father Jesse's flocks. The psalm-songs that David wrote have been proven to be truly prophetic and so co-opted wholesale into Scripture.

While by no means perfect, David is a pivotal figure in Jewish history. Messiah is descended from him - Jesus the son of Joseph, the *'tekton'* associated with training the 1000 priests needed to build the 165 feet tall Holy Place. Jesus therefore continued the Temple building work consigned to David, initially completed by David's son Solomon. This reflects a broader spiritual work of

God that is still active today, as Paul would later describe in Ephesians chapter 2.

13:23-25 'From the descendants of this man, according to promise, God has brought to Israel a Saviour, Jesus, after John had proclaimed before his coming, a baptism of repentance to all the people of Israel. And while John was completing his course, he kept saying, 'What do you suppose that I am? I am not he. But behold, one is coming after me the sandals of whose feet I am not worthy to untie.'

Messiah's coming was steeped in Hebrew prophesy and God's promises therein also contained references to Messiah's forerunner. When John the Baptist had denied that he was 'that prophet' he was referring to Moses' statement that God would send Messiah as 'a prophet like me.' (Deuteronomy 18:15, 'God will raise up for you a prophet like me').

Jesus very clearly fulfilled this important Messianic title. Moses was an intelligent Jew, educated to a high level in Pharaoh's palace, but in a hidden manner, appearing outwardly to be an Egyptian while in reality an Israelite.

Jesus spent some seventeen years graduating as a *'didaskalos'* from the rabbinic training academy that was held in Bet Midrash in the Courts of Israel in the Temple of Herod where the Doctors of Torah gathered to debate and to teach the Law (Luke 2:46). His divine nature was hidden in human form, appearing outwardly to be the son of Joseph and Mary while in reality being the incarnate Son of God.

Moses' mission included being rejected by his own people ("Who made you a ruler and judge over us?") after leaving Pharaoh's palace to free fellow Jews from slavery and the oppression from the brutal Egyptian regime. Jesus was rejected by his own people ("Crucify him!") after leaving the palatial Temple world of scholarship to free fellow Jews from slavery to the oppression of both sin and the many Jewish rabbinic traditions that made up the Oral Law.

Following their rejection both Moses and Jesus returned from exile to set their people free. Moses returned from Midian to set his people free from Egyptian slavery whereas Jesus returned from death to set all men free from slavery to sin.

Jesus' messianic mission was therefore one of the 'Prophet like Moses', running parallel with Moses' in many ways.

13:26-29 'Brethren, sons of Abraham's family, and those among you who fear God, to us the message of this salvation has been sent. For those who live in Jerusalem, and their rulers, recognizing neither him nor the utterances of the prophets which are read every Sabbath, fulfilled these by condemning him. And though they found no ground for putting him to death, they asked Pilate that he be executed .When they had carried out all that was written concerning him, they took him down from the cross and laid him in a tomb.'

The local Jews present that Sabbath morning in Pisidian Antioch were the first of God's covenant people dwelling outside the land of Israel to hear the gospel. And in God's provenance they are hearing it from the lips of Paul, a fellow countryman.

13:30-32 'But God raised him from the dead; and for many days he appeared to those who came up with him from Galilee to Jerusalem, the very ones who are now his witnesses to the people. And we preach to you the good news of the promise made to the fathers.'

Neither Paul nor Barnabas were among Jesus' Galilean disciples, but after his Damascus Road experience Paul could now count himself as being an eye witness of the resurrection. His masterful grasp of the Hebrew Scriptures put him head and shoulders above the rest of the apostles in terms of formal Torah and Scripture scholarship, and more than qualified to proclaim, with them, the *'evangelion'* - the 'good news' of the gospel.

In Jesus one finds that power of forgiveness which sets us free from the condemnation that should have been ours and that therefore restores real friendship with God, one based upon Messiah's sacrifice rather than our own efforts.

13:33-37 'That God has fulfilled this promise to our children in that he raised up Jesus, as it is also written in the second Psalm, `You are my son, today I have begotten you.' As for the fact that he raised him up from the dead, no longer to return to decay, he has spoken in this way: `I will give you the holy and sure blessings of David. Therefore he also says in another Psalm, `You will not allow your holy one to undergo decay. For as David, after he had served the purpose of God in his own generation, fell asleep, and laid among his fathers and underwent decay; but he whom God raised did not undergo decay.'

Jesus' resurrection is explained by a reference to Psalm 16, that death and decay could not destroy the Author of Life. Paul explains that salvation in Messiah is an integral part of the promise God made to David and his descendants, part of these Cypriot Jews' spiritual heritage.

13:38-39 'Therefore let it be known to you, brethren, that through him forgiveness of sins is proclaimed to you, and through him everyone who believes is freed from all things, from which you could not be freed through the Law of Moses.'

The free gift of forgiveness of sin through trusting in Messiah's sacrifice brought not only relief of conscience but also a way out of the never ending cycle of breaching the multiple legal requirements of the rabbinic Oral Law. This is indeed spiritual freedom.

13:40-41 'Therefore take heed, so that the thing spoken of in the Prophets may not come upon you: "Behold you scoffers and marvel, and perish; for I am accomplishing a work in your days, a work which you will never believe, though someone should describe it to you."'

Paul closes by quoting from Habakkuk (1:5), and in particular the Greek rendering given in the Septuagint. Habakkuk is challenging his audience over the impending arrival of the Chaldean army which would destroy the (first) Temple in Jerusalem. This act of devastation served as a God-given sign to the unbelieving people of Israel who would soon find themselves in exile in Babylon.

13:42-43 'As Paul and Barnabas were going out; the people kept begging that these things might be spoken to them the next Sabbath. Now when the meeting of the synagogue had broken up, many of the Jews and of the God-fearing proselytes followed Paul and Barnabas, who, speaking to them, were urging them to continue in the grace of God.'

The unmerited favour of God's grace enabled the both many of the Jews present and also Gentile congregants to open themselves to the good news and in addition, gave them the desire to know more.

13:44-45 'The next Sabbath nearly the whole city assembled to hear the word of the Lord. But when the Jews saw the crowds, they were filled with jealousy and began contradicting the things spoken by Paul, and were blaspheming.'

Evidently not all the religious Jews had attended on the previous Sabbath, or were, at least, unaware of the wider spiritual hunger, especially among the (uncircumcised) God-fearing Gentiles that Paul's gospel presentation had awakened.

Some may have been Jewish women married to men in positions of civil power who were easily able to stir up trouble via their gentile husbands (verse 50).

'Blaspheming' is *'blasphêmeô'*, meaning to 'slander by speaking against', especially disrespectfully or reproachfully in an evil manner.

13:46-49 'Paul and Barnabas spoke out boldly and said, "It was necessary that the word of God be spoken to you first; since you repudiate it and judge yourselves unworthy, of eternal life, behold, we are turning to the Gentiles. For so the Lord has commanded us, 'I have placed you as a light for the Gentiles, that you may bring salvation to the ends of the earth,'" When the Gentiles heard this, they began rejoicing and glorifying the word of the Lord; and as many as had been appointed to eternal life believed. And the word of the Lord was being spread through the whole region.'

The Apostles would have been undoubtedly been struck by the enthusiastic response of the many 'God-fearing proselytes' in the local synagogue's congregation to Paul's message of the gospel.

The negativity of the established local Jews served to reinforce the view that the good news of God's grace expressed in Messiah's death and resurrection was not just for Jews but for all of mankind. Since the Jews had rejected it (again), and so proved themselves unworthy of it, the apostles would now turn to the Gentiles, who were welcoming it.

These non-Jews were delighted, expressed in joyful praise, literally 'esteeming it glorious' that God had favoured them in so gracious a manner. Grace inevitably fuels evangelism and it is therefore not surprising that Luke notes the positive impact that was had on the surrounding region of what is modern-day Turkey.

13:50-52 'But the Jews incited the devout women of prominence and the leading men of the city, and instigated a persecution against Paul and Barnabas, and drove them out of their district. But they shook off the dust of their feet in protest against them and went to Iconium. And the disciples were continually filled with joy and with the Holy Spirit.

Pisidian Antioch was a volatile city, having been established by Alexander the Great in 300 BC as part of his programme of hellenization of the region. In common with all new cities it had proved popular with Jews keen to benefit from the domestic and economic security that such new city ventures offered their communities.

When the Romans took control in 6BC the city consisted of Jews, Greeks and the somewhat highly strung local Phrygians. Because the Jews preached a traditionally high sexual moral standpoint, their synagogues tended to attract women from cultures that took a more lax moral line in relation to marriage.

The Jews could and did exert influence via these women's husbands ('the leading men of the city') to stir up trouble in the form of such vigorous opposition so as to cause the apostles to be forced to leave that place. They resort to the Jewish custom of shaking the dust off their shoes against their antagonists, just as Jesus had taught (Matthew 10:14).

The Jews had long held that the very dust of Gentiles was impure, and was to be shaken off to maintain religious purity. Shaking off the dust from the feet, therefore, was a highly significant act, strongly denouncing the city's Jews as impure, profane, and heathen-like, hence unworthy of being instructed by them, to the point that they vehemently declined all further connection with them.

But opposition from important religious people was nothing new to the early believers and the move of the Spirit continued joyfully unabated.

Chapter 14

14:1-2 'In Iconium they entered the synagogue of the Jews together, and spoke in such a manner that a large number of people believed, both of Jews and of Greeks. But the Jews who disbelieved stirred up the minds of the Gentiles and embittered them against the brethren.'

Iconium was some ninety miles from Pisidian Antioch, and was an ancient city believed to be older than Damascus. Arriving there Paul and Barnabas went as was their custom to the Jewish synagogue, where once again the distinguished disciple of Rabbi Gamaliel was offered the opportunity to speak to the congregation.

Luke is emphasising to Theophilus and Rome in general that Paul was continuing Jesus' ministry of preaching 'to the Jew first', and not attempting to establish a new and separate faith, which would have been directly contrary to Roman law.

Once again, many Jews and also God-fearing Greeks believed. And once again the disbelieving Jews, being still spiritually blind and deaf, rejected the good news, actively opposing the proclamation of the gospel in just the same way that the religious hierarchy in Jerusalem (of which Paul had been a part) had previously opposed Jesus' Kingdom message.

The Greek text for 'embittered' is *'kakoo'*, also meaning 'to harm and entreat evil'.

Rome had a great deal of experience of obdurate behaviour on the part of its Jewish subjects, and the Jews' negative reaction described would be very recognisable to the Roman Court.

14:3-4 'Therefore they spent a long time there speaking boldly with reliance upon the Lord, who was testifying to the word of his grace, granting that signs and wonders be done by their hands. But the people of the city were divided; and some, sided with the Jews, and some with the apostles.'

The outpouring of the Spirit continued for some time, enabling miraculous signs and wonders to be performed by the apostles. These failed to persuade the spiritually resistant Jews however, and a division arose.

14:5-7 'And when an attempt was made by both the Gentiles and the Jews with their rulers, to mistreat and to stone them, they became aware of it and fled to the cities of Lycaonia, Lystra and Derbe, and the surrounding region; and there they continued to preach the gospel.'

Lycaonia was the region comprising the cities of Lystra and Derbe. Western Lycaonia was part of Galatia, a region of modern day Turkey that was under Roman rule.

Eastern Lycaonia was not under Roman rule and was called Lycaonia Antiochiana. This bordered the region of Galatia known as Phrygia, which was under Roman rule.

Derbe was a major city on the south-eastern part of the Turkish Lycaonian plain (southern Galatia). It was on the Roman road to Antioch and served an important role as a Roman customs post, being on e of the few cities to be honoured by Emperor Claudius with the title 'Claudian'.

'Attempt' to mistreat the apostles is *'hormê',* meaning a sudden 'onrush' and 'assault'. Violent and tumultuous actions were common in a part of the region where Roman law and order existed in theory but was thin on the ground in reality, and the local Phrygian's tempers were readily riled up by the resident religious Jews. When the opposition became openly violent the apostles, rather than appeal to their Rom an legal rights, simply moved on to the neighbouring regions.

14:8-12 'At Lystra a man was sitting who had no strength in his feet, lame from his mother's womb, who had never walked. This man was listening to Paul as he spoke, who, when he had fixed his gaze on him and had seen that he had faith to be made well, said with a loud voice, "Stand upright on your feet." And he leaped up and began to walk. When the crowds saw what Paul had done, they raised their voice, saying in the Lycaonian language, "The gods have become like men and have come down to us." And they began calling Barnabas, Zeus, and Paul, Hermes, because he was the chief speaker.'

Lystra had an ancient legend involving the Greek gods Zeus and Hermes, who came to earth seeking hospitality.

They found no one offered any except an old peasant couple who alone were spared destruction.

When the crippled man was healed via Paul, the highly superstitious locals veered to the side of caution, determined to avoid their predecessors' errors, and instead ascribe Greek-god status to the apostles.

14:13-18 'The priest of Zeus, whose temple was just outside the city, brought oxen and garlands to the gates, and wanted to offer sacrifice with the crowds. But when the apostles Barnabas and Paul heard of it, they tore their robes and rushed out into the crowd, crying out and saying, "Men, why are you doing these things? We are also men of the same nature as you, and preach the gospel to you that you should turn from these vain things to a living God, who made the heaven and the earth and the sea and all that is in them. In the generations gone by he permitted all the nations to go their own ways; and yet he did not leave himself without witness, in that he did good and gave you rains from heaven and fruitful seasons, satisfying your hearts with food and gladness. Even saying these things, with difficulty they restrained the crowds from offering sacrifice to them.'

Intervening to stop the idolatry from continuing, Paul draws from creation imagery to point the pagan crowd towards the one true God. Eventually the superstitious non-Jewish local inhabitants of Lystra are persuaded to desist.

14:19-23 'But Jews came from Antioch and Iconium, and having won over the crowds; they stoned Paul and dragged him out of the city, supposing him to be dead. But while the disciples stood around him, he got up and entered the city. The next day he went away with Barnabas to Derbe. After they had preached the gospel to that city and had made many disciples, they returned to Lystra and to Iconium and to Antioch, strengthening the souls of the disciples, encouraging them to continue in the faith, and saying, "Through many tribulations we must enter the kingdom of God." When they had appointed elders for them in every church, having prayed with fasting, they commended them to the Lord in whom they had believed.'

Once again, hostile Antiochian Jews arrive and succeed in persuading the fickle Lystrans to reverse their sentiments even to the extent of attempting to murder Paul. Lystra was an outlying Roman colony where there was little recourse to civil protection and an (illegal) summary execution is hastily enacted.

This episode of extreme violence against the diminutive Paul may well have been the occasion of his experiencing the 'third heaven' (2 Corinthians 12:3-4) when he was 'caught up into paradise.'

Lystrans would have been all too familiar with dead bodies and there is no indication that they had simply made a mistake in judging him deceased, such that they felt compelled to remove the immediate evidence of their crime against this Roman citizen.

God though himself determines the time and manner of his childrens' demises, and since it was clearly not yet the appointed hour for Paul's departure he simply raised

Paul back to life, possibly in answer to the others' prayers, whereupon Paul simply carried on as if nothing untoward had occurred.

Derbe came next, where again they experienced success in delivering their message of the good news of Messiah. They then simply retraced their steps, drawing on their very recent experiences of hostility to reinforce the cost inherent in discipleship to Jesus.

Appointing more senior believers to positions of responsible oversight was to become normal practice for Paul, as may be seen from his later pastoral letters to Timothy and Titus.

The appointments were made following periods of seeking God's will through prayer and fasting.

Chapter 15

15:1-2 'Some men came down from Judea and began teaching the brethren, "Unless, you are circumcised according to the custom of Moses, you cannot, be saved." And when Paul and Barnabas had great, dissension and debate with them, the brethren determined that Paul and Barnabas and some others of them should go up to Jerusalem to the apostles and elders concerning this issue.'

These men are later identified as 'men of the circumcision', probably converted Pharisees who held that the new Messianic Jewish faith did not relieve the Gentile converts from obeying the laws of Moses, especially in relation to the Old Covenant's sign of circumcision. Paul, himself a Pharisee and an extremely gifted Torah scholar, would clash with them again over the question of circumcising Gentile converts (Galatians 5:12, Titus 1:10).

Unable to resolve the issue, it is decided by the church at Antioch to refer the question to the church elders and original apostles in Jerusalem.

15:3-5 'Therefore, being sent on their way by the church, they were passing through both Phoenicia and Samaria, describing in detail the conversion of the Gentiles, and were bringing great joy to all the brethren. When they arrived at Jerusalem, they were received by the church and the apostles and the elders, and they reported all that God had done with them. But some of the sect of the Pharisees who had believed stood up, saying, "It is necessary to circumcise them and to direct them to observe the Law of Moses."'

Pharisees came in many shades. Paul himself had grown up as a Pharisee (Philippians 3:5) and had, in fact, served as such on the Sanhedrin itself. The Talmud describes seven types of Pharisee and only one is in a positive manner, so Jesus was not alone in his disapproval of their hard heartedness. They were effectively religious lawyers, steeped in the Torah, often to the point of nit-picking legalism.

Along with the priests, many had been converted in the move of the Spirit that had followed the Day of Pentecost outpouring. To them the rite of circumcision was central to the covenant God had made with Moses. The discomfort and actual danger of circumcision was often the main reason why otherwise believing Greek and Roman adult men chose to remain 'God-fearers' rather than become fully fledged (circumcised) Jews.

15:6-11 'The apostles and the elders came together to look into this matter. After there had been much debate, Peter stood up and said to them, "Brethren, you know that in the early days God made a choice among you, that by my mouth the Gentiles would hear the word of the gospel and believe. And God, who knows the heart, testified to them in giving them the Holy Spirit, just as he also did to us; and he made no distinction between us and them, cleansing their hearts by faith. Now therefore why do you put God to the test by placing upon the neck of the disciples a yoke which neither our fathers nor we have been able to bear? But we believe that we are saved through the grace of the Lord Jesus, in the same way as they also are."'

The issue at stake was the place of the Mosaic Law in the New Covenant. The Pharisees clung to it as being what defined Judaism but the matter was not simple to determine. It would take very many years for what Peter declared here to become accepted by more traditional, conservative minded Jewish believers such as converted Pharisees.

Paul had earlier written to the church in Rome (Romans 2:25) that 'circumcision has value to one who keeps the law' (given to Moses by the pre-incarnate Jesus on Mount Sinai), and also that the Jewish faith had 'much value in every way' (Romans 3:2).

The New Covenant, based upon faith in Messiah's sacrificial death and resurrection, entailed the hidden sign of a circumcised heart (Romans 2:29) rather than simply the outward physical act performed upon eight day old male Jewish infants.

15:12-21 'All the people kept silent, and they were listening to Barnabas and Paul as they were relating what signs and wonders God had done through them among the Gentiles. After they had stopped speaking, James answered, saying, "Brethren, listen to me. Simeon has related how God first concerned himself about taking from among the Gentiles a people for his name. With this the words of the Prophets agree, just as it is written, after these things I will return, and I will rebuild the tabernacle of David which has fallen, and I will rebuild its ruins, and I will restore it, so that the rest of mankind may seek the Lord and all the Gentiles who are called by my name, says the Lord, who makes these things known from long ago. Therefore it is my judgment that we do not trouble those who are turning to God from among the Gentiles, but that we write to them that they abstain from things contaminated by idols and from fornication and from what is strangled and from blood. For Moses from ancient generations has in every city those who preach him, since he is read in the synagogues every Sabbath.'"

Peter had been the original leader of the early church, however this role had later become devolved to Jesus' devout half-brother James ('the Just'), whose Hebrew name was Jacob. Peter was clearly of the view that the male Gentile converts should not be burdened with the uncomfortable and rather hazardous business of adult circumcision.

James took a slightly more diplomatic view, acknowledging the traditional place of the Mosaic Law, (citing Amos 9:11-12) and giving a deferential nod to what were in fact widely acknowledged reasonable steps - abstaining from idolatry, fornication and eating meat with the blood undrained (contrary to Leviticus 17:14 which teaches that 'the life is in the blood').

These proved sadly insufficient to placate what became known as 'the party of the circumcision', who like the

Jews at Lystra would continue to dog Paul's ministry with their entrenched, legalistic and contrary views.

As Paul would later write: "You were running well; who hindered you from obeying the truth? This persuasion did not come from Him who calls you. A little leaven leavens the whole lump of dough. I have confidence in you in the Lord that you will adopt no other view; but the one who is disturbing you will bear his judgment, whoever, he is. But I, brethren, if I still preach circumcision, why am I still persecuted? Then the stumbling block of the cross has been abolished. I wish that those who are troubling you would even mutilate themselves.' (Galatians 5: 7-12).

15:22-26 'Then it seemed good to the apostles and the elders, with the whole church, to choose men from among them to send to Antioch with Paul and Barnabas - Judas called Barsabbas, and Silas, leading men among the brethren, and they sent this letter by them: 'The apostles and the brethren who are elders, to the brethren in Antioch and Syria and Cilicia who are from the Gentiles, greetings. Since we have heard that some of our number to whom we gave no instruction have disturbed you with their words, unsettling your souls, it seemed good to us, having become of one mind, to select men to send to you with our beloved Barnabas and Paul, men who have risked their lives for the name of our Lord Jesus Christ.'

The Jerusalem based Apostles selected two men, Judas and Silas, to accompany Paul and Barnabas and to represent their letter's contents back in Antioch in Syria.

The letter demonstrates the depth of feeling of Jesus' disciples' unhappiness with what these 'men from James' had done, ostensibly in all of the Apostles' names, in misrepresenting their views on Jewish law to the new daughter church in Syria.

These converted Pharisees had acted 'without instruction' and hence without authority and they had in consequence 'disturbed' the church, this being *'tarasso'*, literally meaning to 'stir up and trouble', which was resulting in an 'unsettling' (*'anaskeuazô'*) of their souls.

'Anaskeuazo' is a strong and rarely used New Testament term, meaning to 'ransack and dismantle other people's belongings' in the manner of a common thief. The negative and deceptive nature of the behaviour of these former Pharisees is clearly contrasted with the honesty and courage of Paul and Barnabas.

15:27-29 'Therefore we have sent Judas and Silas, who themselves will also report the same things by word of mouth. For it seemed good to the Holy Spirit and to us to lay upon you no greater burden than these essentials: that you abstain from things sacrificed to idols and from blood and from things strangled and from fornication; if you keep yourselves free from such things, you will do well. Farewell.'

The Apostles' letter concludes with briefly mentioning the four points of behaviour that it was recommended that the new mixed Jew and Gentile churches avoid.

15:30-35 'So when they were sent away, they went down to Antioch; and having gathered the congregation together, they delivered the letter. When they had read it, they rejoiced because of its encouragement. Judas and Silas, also being prophets themselves, encouraged and strengthened the brethren with a lengthy message. After they had spent time there, they were sent away from the brethren in peace to those who had sent them out. But it seemed good to Silas to remain there. But Paul and Barnabas stayed in Antioch, teaching and preaching with many others also, the word of the Lord.'

The gathering of the church together to hear the message from Jerusalem was also a good opportunity for prophetic ministry, in the form of forth-telling of God's word. Silas would very soon replace Barnabas as Paul's missionary journey companion.

15:36-38 'After some days Paul said to Barnabas, "Let us return and visit the brethren in every city in which we proclaimed the word of the Lord, and see how they are." Barnabas wanted to take John, called Mark, along with them also. But Paul kept insisting that they should not take him along who had deserted them in Pamphylia and had not gone with them to the work.

Barnabas was John Mark's uncle and was understandably keen to give his nephew a second taste of serving God in missionary work. Paul on the other hand felt that Mark had proved unreliable in Pamphylia (Roman south-central Asia Minor, now dominated by Antalya in Turkey - Acts 13:13), and in consequence the two godly leaders went their separate ways.

15:39-40 'There occurred such a sharp disagreement that they separated from one another, and Barnabas took Mark with him and sailed away to Cyprus. But Paul chose Silas and left, being committed by the brethren to the grace of the Lord. And he was travelling through Syria and Cilicia, strengthening the churches.'

The Greek for 'sharp disagreement' is *'paroxusmos'*, and is perhaps better translated as 'stimulus'. Conflict can be helpful in bringing focus in clarifying priorities, and Barnabas clearly felt called by God to visit his native Cyprus.

This splitting up had the great benefit of effectively doubling their missionary presence, and Paul was able to embark upon his second missionary journey via Syria and Turkey in the company of his fellow Roman citizen and former Jerusalem resident Silas.

Chapter 16

16:1-5 'Paul came also to Derbe and to Lystra. And a disciple was there, named Timothy, the son of a Jewish woman who was a believer, but his father was a Greek, and he was well spoken of by the brethren who were in Lystra and Iconium. Paul wanted this man to go with him; and he took him and circumcised him because of the Jews who were in those parts, for they all knew that his father was a Greek. Now while they were passing through the cities, they were delivering the decrees which had been decided upon by the apostles and elders who were in Jerusalem, for them to observe. So the churches were being strengthened in the faith, and were increasing in number daily.'

Lystra owed its importance, and the attention which Paul paid to it, to the fact that it had been made a Roman colony by Augustus, and was, in the time of Paul's ministry, a center of education. The site of Lystra has been placed at a hill near Khatyn Serai, 18 miles south-southwest of Iconium. The boundary between Phrygia and Lycaonia passed between Iconium and Lystra. The population of Lystra consisted of the local aristocracy of Roman soldiers who formed the garrison of the colony, some Greeks and Jews (including Timothy) and of native Lycaonians.

Paul had almost certainly met Timothy when he passed through Lystra on his first journey. An educated (2 Timothy 3:15), intelligent and rather sensitively empathetic young Jewish man, Timothy had made a very good impression already on Paul.

Himself a senior Torah scholar, Paul appears to already have prayerfully decided to offer Timothy the role of disciple-helper that John-Mark's departure had left vacant.

Timothy was evidently also commended highly by the local church and their regard for him was not misplaced. Much later Paul would write to the church at Philippi, 'Timothy's worth you know, how as a son with a father he has served with me in the gospel' (Philippians 2:22), and to the Corinthians referencing Timothy as his 'beloved son' (1 Corinthians 4:17).

But Timothy was uncircumcised, because his father wasn't Jewish. Paul had just come from the Jerusalem church council that had decided that circumcision was not mandatory for Gentiles coming to faith in Messiah.

However, Judaism is passed via the mother and because Timothy would necessarily be interfacing evangelistically with Jews, Paul advocated for his circumcision. This is in keeping with his later comment to the Corinthians: 'To the Jews I became as a Jew, that I might gain the Jews' (1 Corinthians 9:20). This point is relevant to the Court in Rome since it further evidences that Paul was not seeking to promote a new faith, one completely separate from Judaism.

16:6-10 'They passed through the Phrygian and Galatian region, having been forbidden by the Holy Spirit to speak the word in Asia; and after they came to Mysia, they were trying to go into Bithynia, and the Spirit of Jesus did not permit them; and passing by Mysia, they came down to Troas. A vision appeared to Paul in the night: a man of Macedonia was standing and appealing to him, and saying, "Come over to Macedonia and help us." When he had seen the vision, immediately we sought to go into Macedonia, concluding that God had called us to preach the gospel to them.

Journeying on through central Asia Minor (a very mountainous area of modern day Anatolia with fertile tablelands reaching 4,000 feet in height) the Apostles headed west, through Phrygia into the region known as Galatia (see map):

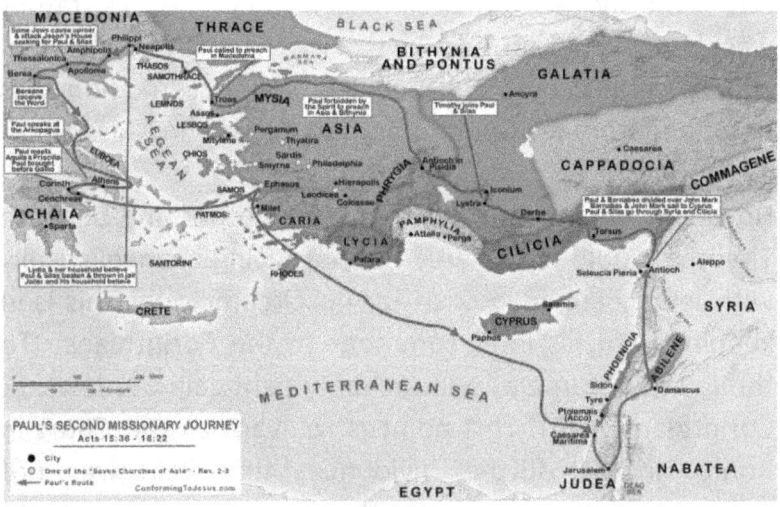

In Roman times, the country was divided into two parts, one known as Galatian Phrygia, and the other as Asian Phrygia, because it was a part of the Roman province of Asia. Asian Phrygia was the larger of the two, including the greater part of the less developed country. Galatian Phrygia was smaller, extending along the Pisidian Mountains. Its established cities included Antioch, Iconium and Apollonia.

Phrygia's name is derived from Phryges, a tribe from Thrace (a region now divided between Bulgaria, Greece and Turkey), which in former times had invaded and either driven out or absorbed the earlier Asiatic inhabitants, among whom were the Hittites. The Phrygians appropriated much culture from oriental civilization, especially art and mythology which was later transferred into Europe.

About 295 AD, when the province of Asia was no longer governmentally kept together, its different parts were known as Phrygia Prima and Phrygia Secunda, and are now ruled by Turkey from Konia (ancient Iconium). The population consists not only of Turks, but also of Greeks, Armenians, Jews, Kurds and many small tribes of uncertain ancestry, and of diverse customs and religious practices.

Luke does not here divulge in what form the Holy Spirit's resistance to movement towards Bithynia manifested itself as. Going there meant heading northeast towards modern Istanbul, the Sea of Marmara, the Bosporos strait and the Black Sea.

Whatever the issues, Paul overcame them by the simple expedient of going to bed, and sleeping on it, whereupon

God guided him further west towards Macedonia supernaturally via a dream of a man in traditional Macedonian dress. Message received and understood, the apostolic missionary team wasted no time in obeying, about-turning their preparations for northeastern movement and travelling northwest instead.

16:11-13 'So putting out to sea from Troas, we ran a straight course to Samothrace, and on the day following to Neapolis, and from there to Philippi, which is a leading city of the district of Macedonia, a Roman colony; and we were staying in this city for some days. And on the Sabbath day we went outside the gate to a riverside, where we were supposing that there would be a place of prayer; and we sat down and began speaking to the women who had assembled.'

Back to Troas then, where Luke had originally joined them, and passage on a boat to Samothrace, a mountainous island in the Aegean Sea, south of Thrace and opposite the mouth of the Hebrus River, northwest of Troas.

Philippi was the leading city of Macedonia, lying on the Egnatian Road, 33 miles from Amphipolis and 21 miles from Acontisma, in a plain bounded on the East and North by the mountains which lie between the rivers Zygactes and Nestus, and bordered to the west by Mount Pangaea, and to the south by the ridge connecting the city with its seaport Neapolis 9 miles southeast. It was a city named after Philip of Macedonia who ruled from 359 BC and who fortified it militarily, enriched by its nearby gold mines and made famous following the Roman conquests of 168 BC for being the location of the battle in 14BC between the forces loyal to the Roman conspirators Brutus and Cassius and those of Octavian (later Caesar Augustus) and Mark Antony that decided the future of Rome as a republic.

Being a Greek-Roman colony there was no synagogue, so the apostles looked for an audience near a river, that being the next most likely location for spiritually receptive people.

16:14-15 'A woman named Lydia, from the city of Thyatira, a seller of purple fabrics, a worshiper of God, was listening; and the Lord opened her heart to respond to the things spoken by Paul. And when she and her household had been baptized, she urged us, saying, "If you have judged me to be faithful to the Lord, come into my house and stay." And she prevailed upon us.'

Led once more by the Spirit, a divine appointment materialises, one resulting in the first European convert to the new faith of Messianic Judaism. Grace prevailed further with a ripple effect bringing her entire household to faith and water baptism. A bold, educated and wealthy woman, she made the most of this graced moment by accommodating the apostolic team, thereby securing Paul's further discipleship and teaching input.

16:16-18 'It happened that as we were going to the place of prayer, a slave-girl having a spirit of divination met us, who was bringing her masters much profit by fortune-telling. Following after Paul and us, she kept crying out, saying, "These men are bond-servants of the Most High God, who are proclaiming to you the way of salvation." She continued doing this for many days. But Paul was greatly annoyed, and turned and said to the spirit, "I command you in the name of Jesus Christ to come out of her!" And it came out at that very moment.'

While walking to the riverbank another spiritual encounter occurs, only this time with an agent of darkness offering some unwanted publicity. The NASB translation quoted above delivers a rare mistranslation - the slave-girl is actually saying that the apostles are proclaiming '**a** way of salvation', not '**the** way of salvation'.

The Greek reads: *'kataggellô hodos'*, where *'hodos'* means 'a highway' (Vine's Expository Dictionary). The significance is not simply the grammatical choice of definite article employed, but the downplaying of the unique spiritual significance of the Gospel message that Paul was relaying.

This, added to his spirit's inner witness, triggers Paul's angry confrontation with the demon at work behind the unlooked for endorsement.

16:19-21 'But when her masters saw that their hope of profit was gone, they seized Paul and Silas and dragged them into the market place before the authorities, and when they had brought them to the chief magistrates, they said, "These men are throwing our city into confusion, being Jews, and are proclaiming customs which it is not lawful for us to accept or to observe, being Romans.'"

In an instant the demonised slave-girl went from being a valuable asset to being almost worthless to her profit obsessed masters. Her new found emancipation from the controlling power of the evil spirit was of no interest to them and was certainly of no fiscal benefit.

Furious at the sudden and unexpected loss of income, the men resort to a vengeful aggression quite possibly aggravated further by an underlying anti-Semitism. They complain to the magistrates of 'these Jews' imposing 'unlawful' practices upon their upright Roman ways.

16:22-24 'The crowd rose up together against them, and the chief magistrates tore their robes off them and proceeded to order them to be beaten with rods. When they had struck them with many blows, they threw them into prison, commanding the jailer to guard them securely; and he, having received such a command, threw them into the inner prison and fastened their feet in the stocks.'

Getting beaten with wooden rods would become something of an occupational hazard for Paul - 'three times I was beaten with rods' (1 Corinthians 11:25). A common Roman punishment, the beatings were inflicted by *'lictors',* muscular men unrestrained by the Jewish laws legal limit of 39 blows. 'Many blows' implies a greater number, as does his remark in 2 Corinthians 11 -

'stripes beyond measure', implying well above the Jews' own legal limit.

Imprisoned in the ultra secure inner cell and bound in wooden stocks, ones which quite possibly forcing the apostles to lie upon their injured backs, they respond by singing praise to God.

16:25-26 'But about midnight Paul and Silas were praying and singing hymns of praise to God, and the prisoners were listening to them; and suddenly there came a great earthquake, so that the foundations of the prison house were shaken; and immediately all the doors were opened and everyone's chains were unfastened.'

God's response to their prayers and praises was to send an earthquake, thus shaking and effectually loosening all of the prisoners' chains and wakening the resident jailer, who as a middle class Roman becomes the third local inhabitant to be opened to the gospel after the poor slave-girl and the upper class Lydia.

Roman law demanded that allowing prisoners to escape brought their punishment upon the errant guard, as seen in the case of Peter's Roman guards (Acts 12), executed by Agrippa after the angel's nocturnal visit. Assuming the worst, the jailer moves to kill himself, only to be stopped by Paul's hasty shout of explanation.

16:28-30 'But Paul cried out with a loud voice, saying, "Do not harm yourself, for we are all here!" And he called for lights and rushed in, and trembling with fear he fell down before Paul and Silas, and after he brought them out, he said, "Sirs, what must I do to be saved?"'

Once again, the Holy Spirit, having done all the hard work, presents the apostles with fruit that is ready to be picked.

16:31-34 'They said, "Believe in the Lord Jesus, and you will be saved, you and your household." And they spoke the word of the Lord to him together with all who were in his house. And he took them that very hour of the night and washed their wounds, and immediately he was baptized, he and all his household. And he brought them into his house and set food before them, and rejoiced greatly, having believed in God with his whole household.'

Paul and Silas presented a message of salvation from Scripture to support the jailer putting trust in Messiah for salvation. The jailer then sets about evidencing his newfound faith by caring practically for the apostles' needs, bringing his whole family to faith and baptism in their turn.

'Baptism' for first century Jews was a process similar to the modern farming practice of dipping sheep. It involved descending into a pool, immersing oneself and then exiting from the opposite side. John the Baptist had baptised Jews in the Jordan River as a mark of their turning from sin.

The Greek word used here is the typical one; *'baptizô'*, in common term for immersion, used in relation to dyeing cloth, pickling vegetables by soaking in vinegar, ship wrecks and even a Spartan army sword initiation ritual. It meant 'to immerse something in something else so as to cause an irreversible (permanent) change in its nature, as opposed to *'bapto'*, meaning 'to dip' - a temporary change only. That sufficient water was available for immersion is evidenced by the quantity having been used immediately previously to wash the apostles' wounds.

The Hebrew practice was also widely used as part of a variety of ritual purifications (e.g. Mark 7:4) and particularly of Jewish worshippers' wholly dipping themselves bodily as part of their spiritual preparation for entry into the Temple Courts in Jerusalem.

In the jailer's home in Philippi the fact that the whole household first believed Paul's message indicates that all present were old enough to comprehend the gospel with an understanding of what they were doing in responding to 'the word of the Lord'. This is further evidenced by the reference to their collective rejoicing.

There is nothing in the passage to support the later (Gentile) church practice of baptising very young infants, something wholly unknown in Jewish tradition.

Paul consistently likened baptism to a wholesale 'burial' of the sinful nature (Romans 6:4, Colossians 2:12), followed by a 'rising' something evidently incompatible with a mere sprinkling or even a partial dipping.

16:35-40 'Now when day came, the chief magistrates sent their policemen, saying, "Release those men." And the jailer reported these words to Paul, saying, "The chief magistrates have sent to release you. Therefore come out now and go in peace." But Paul said to them, "They have beaten us in public without trial, men who are Romans, and have thrown us into prison; and now are they sending us away secretly? No indeed! But let them come themselves and bring us out." The policemen reported these words to the chief magistrates. They were afraid when they heard that they were Romans, and they came and appealed to them, and when they had brought them out, they kept begging them to leave the city. They went out of the prison and entered the house of Lydia, and when they saw the brethren, they encouraged them and departed.'

Some ancient manuscripts read, 'after the earthquake the magistrates sent officers.' Romans regarded earthquakes as significant omens of impending divine judgment and the local magistrates would have had become uneasy with what they surely knew to be a gross abuse of their delegated legal authority. On learning of the apostles' actual Roman citizenship the magistrates even resort to 'begging', something Paul is completely unimpressed by, preferring instead to strengthen the infant church meeting in Lydia's home prior to leaving Philippi.

Once again Luke holds up to the Roman Court Paul's blameless behaviour even in the face of significant civil legal abuses in a region ostensibly under Roman rule.

Chapter 17

17:1-3 'Now when they had travelled through Amphipolis and Apollonia, they came to Thessalonica, where there was a synagogue of the Jews. And according to Paul's custom, he went to them, and for three Sabbaths reasoned with them from the Scriptures, explaining and giving evidence that the Christ had to suffer and rise again from the dead, and saying, "This Jesus whom I am proclaiming to you is the Christ."

Amphipolis was the Roman's capital city of the eastern province of Macedonia, situated near Thrace at the mouth of the River Strymon, which flowed 'around the city' ('*amphi*'), hence occasioning the name Amphi-polis. Philippi was 33 Roman miles from Amphipolis; Amphipolis 30 miles from Apollonia; and Apollonia 37 miles from Thessalonica. Distance was certainly of no object to Paul in the completion of his apostolic mission. The text does not detail Paul's means of travel, other than his cavalry accompanied horse riding journey to Caesarea (Acts 23).

The common scholastic assumption is that he otherwise walked, however several texts point to his relative wealth. Having recently traversed his extensive Asian route myself, and given the abundance of horses prevalent in Asia Minor at the time, I believe it far more likely that he and his companions rode, something Luke clearly states that Paul was well able to do (Acts 23:24).

Fortunately for the Apostolic team the Roman army had constructed a large Roman road (the Egnatian Way) running west-east from the Adriatic Sea to the Middle East which formed Thessalonica's main street.

Thessalonica (also called 'Saloniki' was the main seaport of the second province of Macedonia at the head of the bay Thermaicus. It had been made the capital of the second province by Aemilius Paulus, when he divided the country into four districts. It was formerly called Therma, but afterwards received the name of Thessalonica, either in honour of Cassander's wife Thessalonica, the daughter of Philip, or in honour of a victory which Philip gained over the armies of Thessaly. When Paul visited, it was inhabited by Greeks, Romans, and Jews.

Paul was doubtless happy to get there because unlike Amphipolis and Apollonia, Thessalonica had a synagogue. Paul had developed a ministerial pattern of taking his message about Messiah's birth, life, death and subsequent resurrection to wherever he could find a Jewish-friendly audience, most commonly in a synagogue. The Greek term here is *'h'sunagwgh'*, more accurately, **the** synagogue, indicating their relative scarcity.

Paul has by this stage honed down his gospel message to the following salient points:

1) Messiah's coming was specifically and accurately foretold by the Old Testament prophets, and Jesus

of Nazareth fulfilled all of their many and detailed points to the letter.

2) Messiah would not come initially as a triumphant king, but as a suffering servant-teacher, who would end up being rejected and crucified.
3) Once dead, Messiah would be bodily restored to life after three days.

Paul would faithfully deliver this message on multiple occasions, and on this one in particular, emphasizes that there was a necessity in Messiah's dying, as Jesus of Nazareth had done. Messiah was expected by the Jews, as comprehensively predicted in their Scriptures, and was destined to suffer, not simply triumph.

A suffering Messiah was something that the Jews were and are still generally unwilling to recognise and admit the validity of. However, it was essential to Paul's message of defining and proving that Jesus was the Messiah, which rested upon the Scriptures foretelling that Messiah should die for the sins of mankind.

17:4-5 'Some of them were persuaded and joined Paul and Silas, along with a large number of the God-fearing Greeks and a number of the leading women. But the Jews, becoming jealous and taking along some wicked men from the market place, formed a mob and set the city in an uproar; and attacking the house of Jason, they were seeking to bring them out to the people.'

Paul's initial evangelistic success only serves to once again draw out the latent envy of the resident Jews, who tended to view the God-fearers as being inherently subservient to them.

This was because Gentiles lacked the genetic link to Abraham that set them, as Jews, apart as the God-ordained keepers of the old covenant relationship with their great patriarch, and of the Hebrew Scriptures. They also prided themselves in their role as custodians of the Law entrusted to Moses on Mount Sinai, and its rabbinic applications. The Jews' failure to develop a faith based relationship and to live as God intended left them spiritually blind and deaf, even to Messiah in person, joining together before Pilate to bay for his death by crucifixion and the release of the condemned bandit Barabbas instead.

So the Thessalonian Jews rally a gang of immoral men, no doubt paid to start the riot that led to the attack on Jason's house, where Paul was apparently lodging. Jason may well be the same man referred to as Paul's relative in Romans 16:21. This would provide an obvious explanation for Paul staying there.

17:6-9 'When they did not find them, they began dragging Jason and some brethren before the city authorities, shouting, "These men who have upset the world have come here also; and Jason has welcomed them, and they all act contrary to the decrees of Caesar, saying that there is another king, Jesus." They stirred up the crowd and the city authorities who heard these things. And when they had received a pledge from Jason and the others, they released them.'

Once again, Luke paints the by now very familiar picture of Paul preaching the Jewish Messiah in a Jewish setting, annoying the Jews thereby and subsequently being taken before Roman authorities for judgment before ultimately being legally acquitted. This recurring theme will continue throughout this 'treatise'. Luke was confident that Roman lawyer-judges in general and Theophilus in particular had sufficient experience of the ways their Jewish subjects frequently behaved, to recognise the very negative pattern emerging, and to similarly find Paul 'not guilty' of breaking any Roman laws.

The rent-a-mob of unemployed ne'er-do-wells does indeed cause sufficient unrest to force an official judicial hearing. Jason is forced to provide security as to the future behaviour of the apostles, who were now obliged to leave town.

17:10-11 'The brethren immediately sent Paul and Silas away by night to Berea, and when they arrived, they went into the synagogue of the Jews. Now these were more noble-minded than those in Thessalonica, for they received the word with great eagerness, examining the Scriptures daily, to see whether these things were so.'

Berea was a town near Mount Cithanes sixty mile west of Thessalonica, in what was Macedonia's second province. Here Paul again ministers from the Hebrew Scriptures the message that Messiah would suffer and die. This was something difficult for Jews who were expecting a politically triumphant Messiah to accept. A crucified man was considered as having been cursed by God (Deuteronomy 21:23, Galatians 3:13).

17:13-16 'But when the Jews of Thessalonica found out that the word of God had been proclaimed by Paul in Berea also, they came there as well, agitating and stirring up the crowds. Then immediately the brethren sent Paul out to go as far as the sea; and Silas and Timothy remained there. Now those who escorted Paul brought him as far as Athens; and receiving a command for Silas and Timothy to come to him as soon as possible, they left.'

The all too familiar pattern of being pursued by jealous, angry religious Jews is repeated. The fledgling church respond by wasting no time in moving Paul away, further demonstrating nobility of nature and respect for Paul's senior Jewish social and religious status by accompanying the team to the nearest port, thereby facilitating their forward movement focus. They even sent an escort to ensure that Paul arrived safely at his next destination, Athens.

17:16-17 'Now while Paul was waiting for them at Athens, his spirit was being provoked within him as he was observing the city full of idols. So he was reasoning in the synagogue with the Jews and the God-fearing Gentiles and in the market place every day with those who happened to be present.'

'Full of idols' renders a Greek term not used elsewhere in the New Testament. The idolatrous condition of the city is abundantly testified to by other ancient writers.

For example Pausanias (1 Attica, 1, 24) writes, 'The Athenians greatly surpassed others in their zeal for religion.'

Lucian ('Prometheus', tractate 1, 180) records of Athens, 'On every side there are altars, victims, temples, and festivals.' Livy ('The History of Rome' book 45, chapter 27) states that Athens as 'full of the images of gods and men, adorned with every variety of material, and with all the skill of art.'

Silas and Timothy, not being reputed to be as well known or potentially fiery as the Sanhedrin scholar Paul may have been, remained in Berea, presumably teaching and building further upon the Scriptural foundation that Paul had laid there. Paul made the most of his waiting time in Athens' ultra-religious Greek academic centre by continuing to share the Gospel message, firstly, as was now customary, in the local synagogue.

Later in this, his first largely Gentile city's evangelistic setting, he would try a different, non-Hebrew Scripture and non miraculous sign based ministry approach. His initial somewhat academic philosophical reasoning, met with only limited success.

17:18-21 'And also some of the Epicurean and Stoic philosophers were conversing with him. Some were saying, "What would this idle babbler wish to say?" Others: "he seems to be a proclaimer of strange deities," - because he was preaching Jesus and the resurrection. And they took him and brought him to the Areopagus, saying, "May we know what this new teaching is which you are proclaiming? For you are bringing some strange things to our ears; so we want to know what these things mean." (Now all the Athenians and the strangers visiting there used to spend their time in nothing other than telling or hearing something new.)'

The Greek philosopher Epicurius (341-270 BC) had taught that life's goals were to live tranquilly, without pain or fear, in what was an essentially random existence. He had many disciples, some of whom had encountered Paul, and were distinctly underwhelmed, perhaps misinterpreting his words as denoting two foreign deities; both Jesus and also a feminine deity named 'resurrection' (Greek, *'anastasia'* - literally, 'she who will rise again').

Stoics were also prevalent in Athens - a school of philosophers named from the Greek *'stoa'*, (meaning 'porch'), because Zeno, their founder, had held his school and taught from a porch in Athens. Zeno taught that the Universe was created by God but that all things were fixed by fate. He believed that even God was under the dominion of fatal necessity; that the 'fates' were to be submitted to, and that human passions and affections were to be suppressed and restrained, while happiness consisted in the insensibility of the soul to pain and that men should gain absolute mastery over all the passions and affections of human nature. Stoics were strict concerning virtues, and like the Jewish Pharisees, prided themselves on their own righteousness.

They held that matter was eternal, and that all things were a part of God. They fluctuated in their views of a future state; some of them holding that the soul would exist only until the destruction of the universe, while others believed that it would finally be absorbed into the Divine Essence, and become a part of God.

Paul encountered both groups of philosophers but made little headway. He is described as *'spermologos'*, literally meaning 'a seed picker' - metaphorically someone who picks through rubbish looking for scraps to sell. It was used to denote a parasitic babbler and was extremely uncomplimentary.

17:19-21 'And they took him and brought him to the Areopagus, saying, "May we know what this new teaching is which you are proclaiming? "For you are bringing some strange things to our ears; so we want to know what these things mean." (Now all the Athenians and the strangers visiting there used to spend their time in nothing other than telling or hearing something new.)

The Areopagus is Athens' Mars Hill, where the governing body sat. It was located on a rocky outcrop hill at the western end of the Acropolis in the middle of Athens and met in formal session monthly for three successive nights to decide moral, civil and religious issues.

There is nothing to suggest that Paul's hearing before them was anything more than a genuine interest in what to the Athenians was a 'new faith' message. Paul was widely recognised as a Jewish Torah scholar and was a respected Pharisee, and he is treated deferentially as such throughout, despite his failure to persuade many Athenians of the truth of the gospel.

These Greek rulers' spiritual curiosity was regularly described in antiquity. Thucydides (460-400BC) stated, 'Athenians care for nothing else but to tell or to hear something new.'

17:22-23 So Paul stood in the midst of the Areopagus and said, "Men of Athens, I observe that you are very religious in all respects. "For while I was passing through and examining the objects of your worship, I also found an altar with this inscription, 'To an unknown God.' Therefore what you worship in ignorance, this I proclaim to you,'

Paul adopts a 'comparative religion' approach to his preaching given the disjointed nature of his audience to the Hebrew Scriptures in general and to resurrection in particular. Athens contained hundreds of different altars, including a catch-all one to the God that remained 'unknown' to the Athenians.

Six hundred years beforehand a plague had afflicted the city and a Cretan poet, Epimenides, had proposed that a flock of black and white sheep be let loose throughout the city from the Areopagus. Wherever each lay down it was sacrificed on the nearest altar and if a sheep lay down near the shrine of no known god it was sacrificed to 'The Unknown God.' Paul takes his starting point from this historic situation, of which sight of this particular altar must have reminded him.

Paul hadn't yet discovered that the intellectual complacency of this highly educated Greek audience, combined with their comparative ignorance of both Hebrew Scripture and Judaism, while providing a welcome safe place from hostile Jews within which to proclaim God's word, would make this quite probably his least successful missionary stop on record. Indeed, the lack of response in Athens appears to have clarified his later approach, in Corinth, to communicating the Messianic good news in the same way that Jesus had, with a combination of both spiritual truths and the miraculous.

When writing later to the congregation planted by him at Corinth, he was clear that the 'wisdom of this world' (exactly summing up Athenians as the 'debaters of this age'- 1Corinthians 1:21) led the world to remain in unbelief, and that he had come to Corinth reliant wholly on the saving power of God's word and the spiritual wisdom it so perfectly embodied.

17:24-31 'The God who made the world and all things in it, since he is Lord of heaven and earth, does not dwell in temples made with hands; nor is he served by human hands, as though he needed anything, since he himself gives to all people life and breath and all things; and he made from one man every nation of mankind to live on all the face of the earth, having determined their appointed times and the boundaries of their habitation, that they would seek God, if perhaps they might grope for him and find him, though, he is not far from each one of us; for in him we live and move and exist, as even some of your own poets have said, 'For we also are his children.' Being then the children of God, we ought not to think that the divine nature is like gold or silver or stone, an image formed by the art and thought of man. Therefore having overlooked the times of ignorance, God is now declaring to men that all people everywhere should repent, because he has fixed a day in which he will judge the world in righteousness through a man whom he has appointed, having furnished proof to all men by raising him from the dead."

Paul again prefaces his message by presenting God as the Creator and author of life who has made himself knowable to those whom he formed in his own image. The process of knowing God is one requiring our own initiative in seeking in order that we might find and be found by him. Contrary to the view of the Epicureans, matter is not random; rather there is an underlying design at work. And where there are designs, there must necessarily be a designer.

Paul draws upon the Athenians own culture and beliefs, attempting to bring his audience closer to a Hebrew scriptural worldview.

'For we are also his offspring' is found in 'Phaenomena' by the Greek poet Aratus of Cilicia, the native place of Paul, who wrote about 277 BC. As Paul was from Cilicia, it is probable he was acquainted with Aratus' writings.

The line Paul quotes was expressing something opposite to the views of the Epicureans; and evidences Paul's all round literary skills. Paul then paraphrases a Hebrew perspective opposing idolatry from Isaiah 40:18-23. He concludes by referencing Jesus' bodily resurrection and a call to repentance ('*metanoeô*', meaning to change the mind/thinking) and to forsake the spiritual ignorance of the Greeks' idolatry.

17:32-34 'Now when they heard of the resurrection of the dead, some began to sneer, but others said, "We shall hear you again concerning this." So Paul went out of their midst. But some men joined him and believed, among whom also were Dionysius the Areopagite and a woman named Damaris and others with them.'

Paul's oratory skills received mixed reviews, from sneering disbelief to an expression of further interest, ranging from Dionysius, one of the elite Athenian judges, to Damaris an Athenian noble woman.

And from these small beginnings, a new congregation arose.

Chapter 18

18:1-4 'After these things he left Athens and went to Corinth. And he found a Jew named Aquila, a native of Pontus, having recently come from Italy with his wife Priscilla, because Claudius had commanded all the Jews to leave Rome. He came to them, and because he was of the same trade, he stayed with them and they were working, for by trade they were tent-makers. And he was reasoning in the synagogue every Sabbath and trying to persuade Jews and Greeks'.

Paul's next stop was Corinth, a key city located where Greece is almost cut in two by the Saronic Gulf with its port of Cenchreae on the eastern side and on the other by the Corinthian Gulf with its port Lechaeum. Between the two exists a neck of land less than five miles across and upon that was located the city of Corinth.

All north and south land traffic in Greece had to pass through Corinth because there was no other route available. As a consequence of this Corinth was often referred to as 'The Bridge of Greece'. The alternative sea voyage round the southern extremity of Greece was perilous. The southernmost cape - Cape Malea was the local equivalent of Cape Horn, an extremely hazardous sea route. The Greeks had a proverb, 'Let him who thinks of sailing round Cape Malea first make his will.'

Consequently the east to west trade of the Mediterranean also passed through Corinth, for traders chose that way rather than take the perilous ocean detour round Malea. The enhanced movement of goods through Corinth therefore gave it the reputation as being 'The market place of Greece.' And Corinth was more than just a great commercial centre. She was also home to the Isthmian Games, at that time itself second in reputation only to the Roman's Olympic Games.

But Corinth was also a very sinful city. Paul would later write to the church he planted there: 'Do you not know that the unrighteous will not inherit the kingdom of God? Do not be deceived; neither the immoral, nor idolaters, nor adulterers, nor homosexuals, nor thieves, nor the greedy, nor drunkards, nor revilers, nor robbers will inherit the kingdom of God. And such were some of you.' (1 Corinthians 6:9-11).

The Greeks had a verb meaning 'to play the Corinthian', which stood for a life of lust and debauchery; in Greece if ever a Corinthian was shown on the stage he was always portrayed as being drunk. In more recent (Regency) times the term 'Corinthian' in English use came to mean a reckless, roistering young man.

Located alongside Corinth was the hill of the Acropolis - both a fortress and a temple of the Greek goddess Aphrodite. At its peak the temple had one thousand sacred prostitute priestesses of Aphrodite. In the evenings these women left the temple to come down to the city streets and ply their immoral trade, such that there was a common proverb: 'Not every man can afford a journey to Corinth.'

At this point the Roman Jewish married couple Priscilla and Aquila enter Luke's narrative, having been recently evicted from their home in Rome by the Emperor Claudius (41-54 AD.

The notion of 'tent-maker' as defining Paul's secular occupation has been part of the accepted historic (Gentile) picture for so long that the term has even entered the mainstream English language, denoting any paying side-line occupation that allows an individual to financially support his or her own self in doing whatever they believe to be their God-given main raison d'être.

The Greek term translated as 'tent maker' here is *'skênopoios'*, meaning someone who manufactures the small lightweight portable tents used by travellers. These were mostly used by poorer people and commonly known as 'houses of hair'.

'Tent maker' is, sadly, an excellent illustration of the type of mistake most Bible translators make when they fail to distinguish the difference between the very well documented Macedonian Greek (as used in Athens) from the **Judean** *koine* Greek used by the writers of the New Testament and also by their secular contemporary, Josephus Flavius.

Writing in his various secular histories commissioned shortly after on behalf of Rome by the conquering Emperor Vespasian, Josephus' texts are extremely helpful in providing a contemporary textual comparison.

In translating the Scriptures accurately, cultural considerations are vitally important. Firstly, why would conservative, historically orthodox Jews handle the legally unclean (dead) animal skins needed for making such items? Secondly, where are the Scriptural references to Saul/Paul ever having sewn such skins together?

Long after the people of Israel had given up dwelling in tents as homes they continued to pray and worship in tents, and the job of making such prayer tabernacles was one usually performed by very devout Jews, whose personal piety gave their products some additional spiritual credence.

Even today Jews maintain a preference for praying outdoors, often in the privacy of their own prayer tent - their own personal 'tabernacle'.

Paul, together with Pricilla and Aquila, made these tabernacles for sale to fellow religious Jews; hence 'tabernacle maker' is the much more culturally appropriate rendering of *'skênopoios'*.

18:5-8 'But when Silas and Timothy came down from Macedonia, Paul began devoting himself completely to the word, solemnly testifying to the Jews that Jesus was the Christ. But when they resisted and blasphemed, he shook out his garments and said to them, "Your blood be on your own heads! I am clean. From now on I will go to the Gentiles." Then he left there and went to the house of a man named Titius Justus, a worshiper of God, whose house was next to the synagogue. Crispus, the leader of the synagogue, believed in the Lord with all his household and many of the Corinthians when they heard, were believing and being baptized.'

Yet again the Jews rejected the gospel message. Jesus had endorsed the common Jewish custom, demonstrated here by Paul, of expressing renunciation by shaking off dust from one's clothing or feet. 'As for those who do not receive you, as you go out from that city, shake the dust off your feet as a testimony against them.' (Luke 9:5).

Luke will soon document that the Jews in Jerusalem employed the exact same gesture against Paul himself in chapter 22 verse 23.

The prophet Ezekiel (33:1-11) had expressly advised of the consequences of failing to warn people of their own impending judgment. The people might not listen but if they didn't then their blood would be upon their own heads. And so Paul publically repudiates the local unbelieving Jews. 'Going to the Gentiles' involved moving operations as far as to the Roman household immediately next door where he met with the synagogue ruler's now believing family.

This left Crispus' successor (Sosthenes) leading the traditional Jewish services within direct earshot of this, the latest infant church, as evidenced by Paul's comments about people cursing Jesus (1 Corinthians 12:3), a common Jewish liturgical practice at that time and one apparently loudly emanating from the Jew's traditional synagogue immediately next door.

18:9-11 'And the Lord said to Paul in the night by a vision, "Do not be afraid any longer, but go on speaking and do not be silent; for I am with you, and no man will attack you in order to harm you, for I have many people in this city." And he settled there a year and six months, teaching the word of God among them.'

Jesus' timely appearance to Paul that night brought two messages. Firstly, he should not give way to fear, because he was not going to be harmed. Fear is the main enemy of faith/trust, and leaving the synagogue community was a huge step for any religious Jew.

Secondly, Paul was to continue speaking and proclaiming the Gospel's message of the inclusion of Gentiles in God's plan of salvation. The Jews didn't cease from opposing Paul, no doubt with the same threats of violent retribution that he'd previously himself employed against the first believers in Jerusalem. Consequently the risen Jesus personally delivers the encouragement that Paul needed to hear.

18:12-17 'But while Gallio was proconsul of Achaia, the Jews with one accord rose up against Paul and brought him before the judgment seat, saying, "This man persuades men to worship God contrary to the law." But when Paul was about to open his mouth, Gallio said to the Jews, "If it were a matter of wrong or of vicious crime, O Jews, it would be reasonable for me to put up with you; but if there are questions about words and names and your own law, look after it yourselves; I am unwilling, to be a judge of these matters. And he drove them away from the judgment seat. And they all took hold of Sosthenes, the leader of the synagogue, and began beating him in front of the judgment seat. But Gallio was not concerned about any of these things.'

One of Luke's goals in writing to the 'most excellent' Theophilus was to illustrate the various occasions when Paul had been accused unjustly by the Jews and then legally acquitted by the various ruling Roman authorities.

Made proconsul of Achaia in A.D. 53, Lucas Junias **Gallio** Annaenus was the brother of the famous philosopher Seneca, who wrote of him (Quest. Nature 4) : 'Even those who love my brother Gallio to the utmost of their power do not love him enough' and also, 'No mortal, was ever so sweet to any one, as he was to all; and in him there was such a natural power of goodness, that there was no semblance of art or dissimulation.'

Perhaps 'sweet' Gallio had not previously encountered such malevolent religious Jews as those recently come under his oversight in Achaia.

Determined to attempt manipulating their new Roman governor early in his local appointment, the Jews united against Paul bringing a disingenuous claim of subversion mixed in with their true (religious) grievances. But Gallio, despite being regarded as 'sweet' in domestic Roman circles, wasn't having it.

Roman judgment seats were commonly served by sturdy *'lictors'* - men equipped with solid wooden rods, whose job it was to maintain order and administer on-the-spot summary beatings as directed by the judge. These Court officers sprung into vigorous action and started beating the plaintiffs, who vented their frustrations violently upon Sosthenes (Crispus' replacement), presumably because he, as their synagogue's new ruler had been the main organizer of their legal complaints against Paul. Jesus' assurances that Paul was not going to be harmed were therefore born out in reality.

To all of this, Gallio maintains an air of supreme judicial indifference which would certainly be noted by Theophilus, Luke's Roman legal recipient.

Fortunately God seems to have had better plans for Sosthenes, who is later referred to by Paul (1 Corinthians 1:1) as his 'brother'.

18:18-22 'Paul, having remained many days longer, took leave of the brethren and put out to sea for Syria, and with him were Priscilla and Aquila. In Cenchrea he had his hair cut, for he was keeping a vow. They came to Ephesus, and he left them there. Now he himself entered the synagogue and reasoned with the Jews. When they asked him to stay for a longer time, he did not consent, but taking leave of them and saying, "I will return to you again if God wills," he set sail from Ephesus. When he had landed at Caesarea, he went up and greeted the church, and went down to Antioch.'

Paul then crossed back over to Syria with his fellow tabernacle-making and apostolic colleagues Priscilla and Aquila. His continuing affiliation to and observance of his Jewish faith is illustrated here in his taking a Nazirite vow. This meant that for thirty days he neither ate meat nor drank wine; and he allowed his hair to grow. At the end of the thirty days he made certain offerings in the Temple, whereupon his hair was cut again and the newly regrown hair was burned on the altar as a thanksgiving offering to God.

18:24-28 'Now a Jew named Apollos, an Alexandrian by birth, an eloquent man, came to Ephesus; and he was mighty in the Scriptures. This man had been instructed in the way of the Lord; and being fervent in spirit, he was speaking and teaching accurately the things concerning Jesus, being acquainted only with the baptism of John; and he began to speak out boldly in the synagogue. But when Priscilla and Aquila heard him, they took him aside and explained to him the way of God more accurately. And when he wanted to go across to Achaia, the brethren encouraged him and wrote to the disciples to welcome him; and when he had arrived, he greatly helped those who had believed through grace, for he powerfully refuted the Jews in public, demonstrating by the Scriptures that Jesus was the Christ.'

Alexandria in Egypt was, like Athens, a noted centre of learning in its own right. Home at this time to a million diaspora Jews, it had become a major centre for higher Jewish Scripture studies (particularly allegory) and was also home to serious traditional Jewish scholars such as those who had disputed with Stephen in Acts 6:9.

Apollos appears to have been a convert from this category, a learned, zealous Jew happily untainted by both the spiritual pride and blindness that Jerusalem's Pharisees suffered from and also the complacency and corruption of the ruling Judean priests. All of which had made him fertile ground for the seed of the gospel.

There was one small problem, which was that for all his great learning and appetite for Scripture, he had not progressed to an understanding or experience of the Messiah's identity or the fullness of the Holy Spirit. This was soon remedied by Priscilla and Aquila, and he proved to be just the sort of man to take the gospel message back to the recalcitrant Jews of Achaia, able to categorically prove from their Hebrew Scriptures that Jesus' messianic claims were true. His great learning, combined with a holy *'zeo'* ('zeal', literally a 'boiling fervency' of spirit) proved too great for the Jews who had so strongly opposed Paul in Achaia. Apollos could prove beyond all reasonable doubt the identity of Jesus as the promised Messiah, once Priscilla and Aquila had completed his understanding of the biblical necessity of Messiah's suffering, sacrificial death and resurrection.

The Greek here is *'epideiknumi'*, literally meaning that Apollos 'confuted powerfully', and in a sense that implies moral fault with those Jews being so refuted.

Hence the Alexandrian Jew Apollos quickly established himself as being very similar in both ministry and general temperament to the Roman (Turkish) Jew Paul himself.

He was such an effective communicator of the Gospel that he is recorded as having a great impact upon the fledgling mixed Jew and Gentile congregation in Corinth.

As Paul would soon write: 'What then is Apollos? And what is Paul? Servants through whom you believed, even as the Lord gave opportunity to each one. I planted, Apollos watered, but God was causing the growth. So then neither the one who plants nor the one who waters is anything, but God who causes the growth. Now he who plants and he who waters are one; but each will receive his own reward according to his own labour.' (1 Corinthians 3:5-8).

Chapter 19

19:1-7 'It happened that while Apollos was at Corinth, Paul passed through the upper country and came to Ephesus, and found some disciples. He said to them, "Did you receive the Holy Spirit when you believed?" And they said to him, "No, we have not even heard whether there is a Holy Spirit." And he said, "Into what then were you baptized? And they said, into John's baptism." Paul said, "John baptized with the baptism of repentance, telling the people to believe in him who was coming after him, that is, in Jesus." When they heard this, they were baptised in the name of the Lord Jesus. And when Paul had laid his hands upon them, the Holy Spirit came on them, and they began speaking with tongues and prophesying. There were in all about twelve men.

And so finally the time appointed by God (Acts 18:21) for Paul to visit Ephesus arrived, where he met believers who, like Apollos, were only familiar with the earlier ministry of Jesus' forerunner John the Baptist, and had not yet put their faith in Jesus as the Messiah nor received the Holy Spirit.

This was a common Jewish scenario in an era when the idea of a crucified Messiah represented being 'cursed' by God (Deuteronomy 21:23). Both John's Gospel and the Letter to the Hebrews were later written largely to address the differences between John and Jesus.

On this occasion Paul is able to easily complete their circle of faith and both water and Spirit baptism quickly follow, the latter being evidenced by spiritual gifts.

Ephesus (named from the Greek meaning 'desirable') was situated strategically (in modern day Turkey) near the mouth of the Cayster River, 3 miles from the western coast of Asia Minor and opposite the Greek island of Samos.

Pergamos was the center of the local Roman region and its government, but Ephesus was a port and so was more accessible, both as a commercial center and with the added attraction of being home to the goddess Diana. The temple of Diana (Artemis) attracted and became an actual store for the region's wealth, eventually acting as a type of bank.

Dating from the time of the Amazons, this massive pagan Temple was seven times destroyed by fire and rebuilt, each time on a scale larger and grander than before. The wealthy king Croesus supplied many of its fine stone columns, and pilgrims from all over the oriental world brought it much wealth in offerings. In time the Temple came to possess valuable lands; it controlled the local fishing, and on account of its immense structural strength local wealthy people entrusted it with storing their money and many of their most valuable possessions. Not only was the temple of Diana a place of worship, and a treasure-house, it was also a museum in which the best statuary and most beautiful paintings of the region were preserved.

Additionally the Temple of Diana/Artemis became a legal sanctuary for criminals, a Greek form of the Hebrew's cities of refuge, where no one could be arrested for any crime whatever when within a bowshot of its walls. Consequently there was surrounding the temple a large village in which thieves and murderers made their homes and lived freely.

The Temple of Diana/Artemis was responsible for vast numbers of pilgrims visiting Ephesus every year. Consequently it became a major source of employment for a large number of local artisans who manufactured images of the goddess Diana, or small shrines to sell to the visitors, rather like the Vatican has to some extent done in more modern times. A thriving trade existed, with many of these products on view today in the Ephesus Museum, near Izmir in Turkey.

With an artificial harbour accessible to large ships at the entrance of the valley into the interior of Asia Minor, and connected by road with the other chief cities of the province, Ephesus was by far the most accessible city in Asia, both by land and sea. Its location between east and west favoured its religious, political and commercial development and therefore was an excellent place for Paul to further his apostolic and evangelistic mission to the Gentiles from. In total he ministered from there for over three years.

19:8 'And he entered the synagogue and continued speaking out boldly for three months, reasoning and persuading them about the Kingdom of God.'

As usual, Paul commenced operations in the local synagogue. And as equally usual, he met with resistance from the local Jews. Jesus had challenged the hardness of heart of the ruling Jews in Judea (Matthew 13:15) and the Ephesians Jews are similarly described here by Luke.

19:9-10 'But when some were becoming hardened and disobedient, speaking evil of the Way before the people, he withdrew from them and took away the disciples, reasoning daily, in the school of Tyrannus. This took place for two years, so that all who lived in Asia heard the word of the Lord, both Jews and Greeks.'

The local religious Jews slandered the new Messianic faith openly, such that Paul separated himself from them, removing himself to the lecture hall of Tyrannus, a local Greek philosopher. At the Ephesians' extended siesta time of 11AM until 4PM, this hall was unoccupied, and Paul freely engaged in daily *'dialegomai'* (a 'reasoned discussion') there with the believers and anyone else who wanted to listen to him, over a two year period.

The large number of pagan visitors to Ephesus ensured a steady flow of enquirers, who, upon being converted, took the gospel message back home with them on returning to their native Asian towns.

19:11-17 'God was performing extraordinary miracles by the hands of Paul, so that handkerchiefs or aprons were even carried from his body to the sick, and the diseases left them and the evil spirits went out. But also some of the Jewish exorcists, who went from place to place, attempted to name over those who had the evil spirits the name of the Lord Jesus, saying, "I adjure you by Jesus whom Paul preaches." Seven sons of one Sceva, a Jewish chief priest, were doing this. And the evil spirit answered and said to them, "I recognize Jesus, and I know about Paul, but who are you?" And the man, in whom was the evil spirit, leaped on them and subdued all of them and overpowered them, so that they fled out of that house naked and wounded. This became known to all, both Jews and Greeks, who lived in Ephesus; and fear fell upon them all and the name of the Lord Jesus was being magnified.'

Paul's diligent ministry of explaining the new messianic faith dimension was supported by an outpouring of signs and wonders reminiscent of Jesus' own ministry in Judea. It was so successful that it even attracted the attention of local Jewish copycats, sons of one of the many chief priests who served as foreign synagogue rulers, a man named Sceva.

Sadly they lacked the necessary spiritual authority to underpin their audacity and came off very much the worse. This too only served to accentuate the impact of Paul's ministry on the local Greek population, resulting in Messiah being 'magnified', meaning to 'make great and celebrated'.

19:18-20 'Many also of those who had believed kept coming, confessing and disclosing their practices. And many of those who practiced magic brought their books together and began burning them in the sight of everyone; and they counted up the price of them and found it fifty thousand pieces of silver. So the word of the Lord was growing mightily and prevailing.'

Occult practices were well known at Ephesus including *'The Ephesian letters',* by which incantations and charms were believed to be produced. This seem to have consisted of certain combinations of letters or words, which, by being pronounced with certain intonations of voice, were believed to be effectual in expelling diseases or evil spirits; or which, by being written on parchment and worn, were supposed to operate as amulet type charms, to guard against evil spirits and danger.

Plutarch (Sympos. 7) says, 'The magicians compel those who are possessed with a demon to recite and pronounce The Ephesian letters, in a certain order, by themselves. Clemens Alexander (Strom 2) says, 'Androcydes, a Pythagorean, says that the letters which are called Ephesian, and which are so celebrated, are symbols.' Erasmus says, (Adagg, Cent. 2) that there were certain marks and magical words among the Ephesians, by using which they succeeded in every undertaking.

Homer's Odyssey states that, 'the letters were incantations which Croesus used when on the funeral pile, and which greatly befriended him.' Homer adds that in the war between the Milesians and Ephesians, the latter were saved thirteen times from ruin by the use of these supposedly magical letters.

The Gentile converts in Ephesus demonstrated their genuine repentance at considerable material loss to themselves, burning these materials publicly. This was a visible sign that the Gospel was *'ischuo'* - 'strong and powerful', hence 'prevailing' over the local occult practices.

19:21-22 'Now after these things were finished, Paul purposed in the Spirit to go to Jerusalem after he had passed through Macedonia and Achaia, saying, "After I have been there, I must also see Rome." And having sent into Macedonia two of those who ministered to him, Timothy and Erastus, he himself stayed in Asia for a while.'

Timothy and Erastus (a city treasurer of Corinth - Romans 16:23) were sent ahead of Paul into Macedonia en route to Jerusalem. Paul's intention was to deliver financial aid from the wealthy Gentile convert churches to the poorer Jewish believers in Jerusalem (Romans 15:25-26).

19:23-27 'About that time there occurred no small disturbance concerning the Way. For a man named Demetrius, a silversmith, who made silver shrines of Artemis, was bringing no little business to the craftsmen; these he gathered together with the workmen of similar trades, and said, "Men, you know that our prosperity depends, upon this business. "You see and hear that not only in Ephesus, but in almost all of Asia, this Paul has persuaded and turned away a considerable number of people, saying that gods made with hands are no gods at all. Not only is there danger that this trade of ours fall into disrepute, but also that the temple of the great goddess Artemis be regarded as worthless and that she whom all of Asia and the world worship will even be dethroned from her magnificence.'"

The Temple of Diana in Ephesus was one of the wonders of the world. A large and profitable trade had grown up selling religious artefacts to pilgrim visitors, including silver representations of the multi-breasted pagan fertility goddess Diana, to whom the city of Ephesus had been dedicated. The Temple of Diana was constructed over a two hundred and twenty year period, and was built at the expense of all Asia Minor.

The original object of worship among the Ephesians was a small statue of the fertility goddess Diana, made of elm or ebony, made by man but popularly believed to have been sent down from heaven by Jupiter. It was an Egyptian hieroglyphic with many breasts, representing the fertility goddess of nature, and Diana was worshipped as such at Ephesus within the Temple of Artemis, the daughter of Zeus and the sister of Apollo.

Artemis was the Greek goddess of hunting, nature and chastity, known to the Romans as Diana. The Temple of Artemis/Diana at Ephesus was twice as large as the Parthenon in Athens and was regarded as one of the seven wonders of the ancient world.

It was repaired and restored on several occasions (mainly as a result of earth tremors along a local fault line) before declining in both spiritual and economic relevance, its lucrative trade having been very severely undermined by the success of Paul's ministry in converting so many of the surrounding Gentiles to faith in Jesus as Messiah.

The final structure was burnt by the Goths in their naval invasion in A.D. 260 and today in Ephesus only some ruins remain.

19:28-41 'When they heard this and were filled with rage, they began crying out, saying, "Great is Artemis of the Ephesians!" The city was filled with the confusion, and they rushed with one accord into the theatre, dragging along Gaius and Aristarchus, Paul's travelling companions from Macedonia. And when Paul wanted to go into the assembly, the disciples would not let him. Also some of the Asiarchs who were friends of his sent to him and repeatedly urged him not to venture, into the theatre. So then, some were shouting one thing and some another, for the assembly was in confusion and the majority did not know for what reason they had come together. Some of the crowd concluded it was Alexander, since the Jews had put him forward; and having motioned with his hand, Alexander was intending to make a defence to the assembly. But when they recognized that he was a Jew, a single outcry arose from them all as they shouted for about two hours, "Great is Artemis of the Ephesians!" After quieting the crowd, the town clerk said, "Men of Ephesus, what man is there after all who does not know that the city of the Ephesians is guardian of the temple of the great Artemis and of the image which fell down from heaven? So, since these are undeniable facts, you ought to keep calm and to do nothing rash. For you have brought these men here who are neither robbers of temples nor blasphemers of our goddess. So then, if Demetrius and the craftsmen who are with him have a complaint against any man, the courts are in session and proconsuls are available; let them bring charges against one another. But if you want anything beyond this, it shall be settled in the lawful assembly. For indeed we are in danger of being accused of a riot in connection with today's events, since there is no real cause for it, and in this connection we will be unable, to account, for this disorderly gathering." After saying this he dismissed the assembly.'

Of particular note in this passage is Luke's reference to 'the Asiarchs'. These men were the Greeks' equivalent of city elders and magistrates. Asiarchs presided over sacred things, including the public games. It was their business to see that the proper services of religion were observed, and that proper honour was rendered to the Roman emperor in the festivals/games, etc. They were annually elected, and their election had to be formally validated in Rome itself. They held common councils at the principal city within their province, e.g. Ephesus, Smyrna, Sardis, etc., to consult and deliberate about the interests committed to their charge in their various provinces. Their counsel indicates that they had heard Paul preach, and were very supportive towards his views and teaching. The legal significance of this would not be lost upon Theophilus in Rome and at Paul's impending trial.

The Greek goddess Diana, though well known in Rome, did not warrant a place in their Parthenon. Luke includes this footnote for Theophilus' benefit to point out once more that his friend Paul had acted in accord with Roman law, in a Roman colony, and been violently accused, by non-Romans, of acts that, even if true, were certainly no breach of Roman law.

The parallels with the Judean Jews later unjust accusations are being clearly drawn by wise Dr Luke - Paul is guilty of nothing remotely like wrongdoing from a Roman legal perspective, and hence should be acquitted.

Demetrius' self-interest based riot was eventually calmed by the city clerk, a Roman appointee probably primarily concerned with his own job security.

He correctly affirms Paul's innocence before dismissing the crowd. This would carry further weight legally with Nero's court in Rome.

Chapter 20

20:1-6 'After the uproar had ceased, Paul sent for the disciples, and when he had exhorted them and taken his leave of them, he left to go to Macedonia. When he had gone through those districts and had given them much exhortation, he came to Greece. And there he spent three months, and when a plot was formed against him by the Jews as he was about to set sail for Syria, he decided, to return through Macedonia. And he was accompanied by Sopater of Berea, the son of Pyrrhus, and by Aristarchus and Secundus of the Thessalonians, and Gaius of Derbe, and Timothy, and Tychicus and Trophimus of Asia. But these had gone on ahead and were waiting for us at Troas. We sailed from Philippi after the days of Unleavened Bread, and came to them at Troas within five days; and there we stayed seven days.'

Paul issued final words of *'parakaleós'* - 'exhortation', 'consolation' and 'comfort' for the Ephesians' strengthening, after which the team headed back into Macedonia, teaching the local communities of believers as they went. Arriving in Greece, their ministry is once again disrupted by the murderous intentions of some local Jews. A 'plot' here is *'epiboule'*, meaning 'a lying in wait' - and not with friendly fraternal greetings in mind.

Sea crossings to Israel pre-festival with personally malevolent pilgrim Jews would very definitely be a risky business; hence Paul abandons his plan of an immediate sea crossing back to Syria and instead retraces his steps back into Macedonia as far as Troas. Troas was the chief

Roman city in the Northwest of Asia Minor, on the coast of Mysia, and had previously been the ancient home of the Seleucid kings. As a Roman citizen Paul would be safer there from any Jewish murderous attentions.

Paul's companions included: Sopater of Berea, who may be the same person who is referred to later as Sosipater (Romans 16:21), there said to have been a kinsman (near relative) of Paul. Aristarthus, and Gaius of Derbe are also mentioned in Acts 19:29. Tychicus, a man high in the confidence and affection of Paul, was later referred to by him as 'a beloved brother, and faithful minister in the Lord' (Ephesians 6:21-22). Trophimus was from Ephesus (Acts 20:29), and is much later referred to as having been unwell at Miletus (2 Timothy 4:20).

These men, who hailed from a variety of church locations, formed a competent and cooperative apostolic team under Paul's oversight.

20:7-12 'On the first day of the week, when we were gathered together to break bread, Paul began talking to them, intending to leave the next day, and he prolonged his message until midnight. There were many lamps in the upper room where we were gathered together. And there was a young man named Eutychus sitting on the window sill, sinking into a deep sleep; and as Paul kept on talking, he was overcome by sleep and fell down from the third floor and was picked up dead. But Paul went down and fell upon him, and after embracing him, he said, "Do not be troubled, for his life is in him." When he had gone back up and had broken the bread and eaten, he talked with them a long while until daybreak, and then left. They took away the boy alive, and were greatly comforted.'

Verse 7 marks the re-entry of Luke ('we') as narrator, and the account is clearly that of an eye-witness.

The early church celebrated a common meal together weekly, usually culminating with a celebration of the Lord's Supper. Many of the church were poor slaves and this would have been the only decent meal they ate all week.

On this occasion Paul took the opportunity to teach. A combination of a hot stuffy room, a full stomach and 'Paul's talking on and on' had an inevitably soporific affect, particularly on young Eutychus who, in slumber, fell to his death from the third floor window ledge on which he was seated. Paul responded to his death in the calm manner of Elisha with the Shunammite widow's son, (2 Kings 4:33-35) and with the same miraculous outcome.

20:13-17 'But we, going ahead to the ship, set sail for Assos, intending from there to take Paul on board; for so he had arranged it, intending himself to go by land. And when he met us at Assos, we took him on board and came to Mitylene. Sailing from there, we arrived the following day opposite Chios; and the next day we crossed over to Samos; and the day following we came to Miletus. For Paul had decided to sail past Ephesus so that he would not have to spend time in Asia; for he was hurrying to be in Jerusalem, if possible, on the day of Pentecost.'

From Troas, Assos (in Epirus) was 20 miles by road whereas it was 30 miles by sea; the sea journey involved the rounding of Cape Lectum against the strong prevailing north-easterly winds. Paul decided to make the shorter journey and to be met by the ship at the port of Assos.

Chios was on the Greek island of Samos, located a short distance south of Ephesus. Mitylene was the capital city of the Greek Mediterranean island of Lesbos and was the ancient capital of Ionia. It was founded in the eleventh century BC originally a colony of the Cretans and was situated 28 miles south of Ephesus at the mouth of the Maeander River (modern-day Izmir in Turkey). From here Paul summoned the Ephesian church elders.

20:17-24 'From Miletus he sent to Ephesus and called to him the elders of the church. And when they had come to him, he said to them, "You yourselves know, from the first day that I set foot in Asia, how I was with you the whole time, serving the Lord with all humility and with tears and with trials which came upon me through the plots of the Jews; how I did not shrink from declaring to you anything that was profitable, and teaching you publicly and from house to house, solemnly testifying to both Jews and Greeks of repentance toward God and faith in our Lord Jesus Christ. And now, behold, bound by the Spirit, I am on my way to Jerusalem, not knowing what will happen to me there, except that the Holy Spirit solemnly testifies to me in every city, saying that bonds and afflictions await me. But I do not consider my life of any account as dear to myself, so that I may finish my course and the ministry which I received from the Lord Jesus, to testify solemnly of the gospel of the grace of God."

There at the port of Miletus on the coast of Caria, near the mouth of the Meander River, whose merchants had founded 75 trading colonies, the apostle knelt to pray with his friends and converts from Ephesus.

What follows is surely one of the most personal and moving passages in the whole of the New Testament, perhaps second only to Jesus' High Priestly prayer in the Gospel of John (chapter 17). In it we see the true heart attitude of the apostle, always a servant, faithful to God and his word, written, orally communicated and more lately become flesh in the person of Messiah.

The apostle served others with humility without regard for his standing as a religious scholar of repute, not to mention also being a Sanhedrin associate from a wealthy and influential Jewish-Roman family.

Paul was not a man devoid of emotion. Weeping and a tender heart characterised his ministry (Acts 20:31, Phil 3:18, 2 Corinthians 2:4), as a response both to sin and the opposition of wicked men. Repentance and faith sum up Paul's message - aligning our minds and our thinking with both Scripture and the Holy Spirit, combined with an attitude of spiritual dependency in absolute trust upon God.

20:25-35 'And now, behold, I know that all of you, among whom I went about preaching the kingdom, will no longer see my face. Therefore, I testify to you this day that I am innocent of the blood of all men. For I did not shrink from declaring to you the whole purpose of God. Be on guard for yourselves and for all the flock, among which the Holy Spirit has made you overseers, to shepherd the church of God which he purchased with his own blood. I know that after my departure savage wolves will come in among you, not sparing the flock; and from among your own selves men will arise, speaking perverse things, to draw away the disciples after them. Therefore be on the alert, remembering that night and day for a period of three years I did not cease to admonish each one with tears. And now I commend you to God and to the word of his grace, which is able to build you up and to give you the inheritance among all those who are sanctified. I have coveted no one's silver or gold or clothes. You yourselves know that these hands ministered to my own needs and to the men who were with me. In everything I showed you that by working hard in this manner you must help the weak and remember the words of the Lord Jesus, that he himself said, `It is more blessed to give than to receive.'"

Having opened up his heart to them, Paul issues some stern warnings. The elders are to guard against 'cruel wolves' from without and perverse speakers from within. 'Perverse' things' spoken/taught *is 'diastrephô'*, meaning to 'make crooked', often by subtle or indeed blatant misinterpretation and misrepresentation.

Nowhere is this plainer today than in the popular rendering of both Jesus' and his father Joseph's Jewish humanity as being that of impoverished and uneducated peasant carpenters, leading to a diminution of Messiah's humanity and a consequential loss of understanding of his words and deeds within Judean first century life.

With the later almost overnight expansion of the western church under Emperor Constantine, the now increasingly Gentile new faith became trivialized to both accommodate and keep subservient the massive influx of citizens as baptized 'converts'. The church thus quickly became an instrument of state control rather than one of genuine personal spiritual regeneration. Truth became very slightly twisted, making it a much more effective vehicle for deception than any outright lie ever could have been.

Paul knew that God himself in general and his word of truth in particular were what the infant church needed. The attitude of the Ephesians was to be one of giving rather than receiving, thereby imitating Jesus' example. What we get enables us to live, whereas it is what we give that enables us to make a life.

20:36-38 'When he had said these things, he knelt, down, and prayed with them all. And they began to weep aloud and embraced Paul, and repeatedly kissed him, grieving especially over the word which he had spoken, that they would not see his face again. And they were accompanying him to the ship.'

After much emotional and heartfelt prayer, Paul was escorted by the Ephesian elders onto the boat for his festival voyage back to Israel.

Chapter 21

21:1-6 'When we had parted from them and had set sail, we ran a straight course to Cos and the next day to Rhodes and from there to Patara; and having found a ship crossing over to Phoenicia, we went aboard and set sail. When we came in sight of Cyprus, leaving it on the left, we kept sailing to Syria and landed at Tyre; for there the ship was to unload its cargo. After looking up the disciples, we stayed there seven days; and they kept telling Paul through the Spirit not to set foot in Jerusalem. When our days there were ended, we left and started on our journey, while they all, with wives and children, escorted us until we were out of the city. After kneeling, down, on the beach and praying, we said farewell to one another. Then we went on board the ship, and they returned home again.

Cos (now Kos) is a small island in the Greek Aegean Sea's Dodecanese archipelago, a short distance from the south-western point of Asia Minor. It was famous for its soil fertility, and for the wine and silk-worms which it produced. From there Paul's ship travelled to Rhodes. On this island, (formerly known as Asteria) was a city also named Rhodes (after the roses cultivated there) and noted for its huge bronze statue of Colossus. This stood across the mouth of the harbour; and was so high that sea-going vessels could pass between its legs. After standing for fifty-six years it was destroyed by an earthquake having previously been considered to be one of the Seven Wonders of the Ancient World.

Phoenecia was what is now Lebanon.

21:7-10 'When we had finished the voyage from Tyre, we arrived at Ptolemais, and after greeting the brethren, we stayed with them for a day. On the next day we left and came to Caesarea, and entering the house of Philip the evangelist, who was one of the seven, we stayed with him. Now this man had four virgin daughters who were prophetesses. As we were staying there for some days, a prophet named Agabus came down from Judea'.

Ptolemais, on the Mediterranean coast, is situated on the north angle of a bay which extends as far as the point of Mount Carmel. It had belonged to the tribe of Asher (Judges 1:31). At the south and west sides it was surrounded by triple walls. It had originally been called Acerio; but was named Ptolemais in honour of one of the officers serving Alexander the Great (Ptolemy I), who had greatly beautified and adorned it. From there the team journeyed on to Caesarea, where the deacon and evangelist Philip resided with his four single ('virgin') daughters. These young women all exercised the gift of prophecy, and were evidently sufficiently well known in Judea to attract visitors similarly gifted, including Agabus.

21:11-14 'And coming to us, he took Paul's belt and bound his own feet and hands, and said, "This is what the Holy Spirit says: 'In this way the Jews at Jerusalem will bind the man who owns this belt and deliver him into the hands of the Gentiles.' When we had heard this, we as well as the local residents began begging him not to go up to Jerusalem. Then Paul answered, "What are you doing, weeping and breaking my heart? For I am ready not only to be bound, but even to die at Jerusalem for the name of the Lord Jesus." And since he would not be persuaded, we fell silent, remarking, "The will of the Lord be done!"'

The ministry of the prophet was a very important one in the life of the early church (see 1 Corinthians 14). Prophets forth-told the *'rhema'* word of God - his specific directional message for a given time and a particular set of circumstances.

Agabus had also appeared earlier (in Acts 11:27), foretelling a severe famine. His dramatic enactment of the treatment that Paul was to receive in Jerusalem simply reinforced Paul's existing knowledge of God's will and did nothing to deter Paul from following what he was convinced was the call on his life.

21:15-17 'After these days we got ready and started on our way up to Jerusalem. Some of the disciples from Caesarea also came with us, taking us to Mnason of Cyprus, a disciple of long standing with whom we were to lodge. After we arrived in Jerusalem, the brethren received us gladly.'

The final leg of the journey to Jerusalem was southwards down the coastal road via the Roman provincial capital city Caesarea Philippi. This stood at the southwest base of Mount Hermon, some 1,150 feet above sea-level. Caesarea Philippi had once been a center for the worship of Pan (the Greek's god of nature) and the name Paneas had been applied not only to the city itself, but to the whole district ('Antiquities', 15, 10, 3).

The region was assigned by the Emperor Augustus to Herod the Great who built a temple of white marble there in honour of the emperor.

Paneas later formed part of the tetrarchy of Herod the Great's son Herod Philip II, who rebuilt and beautified the town, calling it Caesarea as a compliment to Augustus, and adding his own name to distinguish it from the other Caesarea on the coast of Sharon ('Antiquities,' 18,2,1).

21:18-26 'And the following day Paul went in with us to James, and all the elders were present. After he had greeted them, he began to relate one by one the things which God had done among the Gentiles through his ministry. And when they heard it they began glorifying God; and they said to him, "You see, brother, how many thousands there are among the Jews of those who have believed, and they are all zealous for the Law; and they have been told about you, that you are teaching all the Jews who are among the Gentiles to forsake Moses, telling them not to circumcise their children nor to walk according to the customs. What, then, is to be done? They will certainly hear that you have come. Therefore do this that we tell you. We have four men who are under, a vow; take them and purify yourself along with them, and pay their expenses so that they may shave their heads; and all will know that there is nothing to the things which they have been told about you, but that you yourself also walk orderly, keeping the Law. But concerning the Gentiles who have believed, we wrote, having decided that they should abstain from meat sacrificed to idols and from blood and from what is strangled and from fornication." Then Paul took the men, and the next day, purifying himself along with them, went into the temple giving notice of the completion of the days of purification, until the sacrifice was offered for each one of them.'

Paul met with the leaders of the predominantly Jewish messianic congregation in Jerusalem, led by Jesus' half-brother James (Hebrew: 'Jacov' - Jacob).

James was an extremely devout Jew, so learned that he still held the favour of the ruling Pharisees on the Sanhedrin, evidenced by his ability to remain living in Jerusalem during and after the great persecution that arose following the murder of James the Apostle (Acts 4) and which had caused the dispersal of the more rank and file believers.

Jesus' half-brother James' social and religious standing was certainly the direct result of his father Joseph's standing in that society, as a 'master-tekton' likely responsible for training the one thousand priests that Herod the Great had assigned to constructing his Temple in 13BC (see 'The Jesus Discovery - Another Look at Christ's Missing Years').

For centuries scholars have debated whether or not the Jerusalem council of elders' advice to Paul was sound. The key to answering this question is in Luke's purpose in writing to Theophilus. Luke is not primarily concerned with writing about theology or church history, rather, he is providing Theophilus with Paul's legal chronology, the factual **eye-witness** legal evidence needed to clear Paul of the serious allegations made against him, namely that Paul was propagating a new (and therefore illegal) religion under Roman law.

This brought into play the capital offence of sedition, a similar legal scenario to the one that had brought about Jesus' death by crucifixion.

We know that Theophilus succeeded in getting Paul found not guilty of these charges because we know that Clement of Rome recorded that Paul subsequently travelled to the Iberian Peninsula (Spain) with the gospel, as he had already expressed the desire to do (Romans 15:24,28).

Luke is writing to show that Paul was, in fact, still a good Jew. The Jerusalem congregation's elders are giving Paul what seemed, correctly, to them to be their best advice: "Prove that you're a good Jew by offering a Jewish sacrifice in the Temple."

And because Paul **was** still a 'good Jew', he agrees to follow their (good) advice. The outcome of Paul's arrest and his subsequent appeal to Caesar etc, was, of course, already known to God and part of his overall plan for Paul to take the gospel to Rome.

The very fact that Paul was present shaven headed in the Temple categorically proved that Paul was still a 'good Jew', one lawfully practising Judaism as a good Roman citizen. And the Roman Court (under Emperor Nero) later agreed.

21:27-32 'When the seven days were almost over, the Jews from Asia, upon seeing him in the temple, began to stir up all the crowd and laid hands on him, crying out, "Men of Israel, come to our aid! This is the man who preaches to all men everywhere against our people and the Law and this place; and besides he has even brought Greeks into the temple and has defiled this holy place." For they had previously seen Trophimus the Ephesian in the city with him, and they supposed that Paul had brought him into the temple. Then all the city was provoked, and the people rushed together, and taking hold of Paul they dragged him out of the temple, and immediately the doors were shut. While they were seeking to kill him, a report came up to the commander of the Roman cohort that all Jerusalem was in confusion. At once he took along some soldiers and centurions and ran down to them; and when they saw the commander and the soldiers, they stopped beating Paul.'

'Asia' refers to the Roman province of western Asia Minor, corresponding with modern day Turkey, the area Paul had very recently left, after having had great success in Ephesus. They accused Paul of bringing a non-Jew into the Temple, something strictly forbidden, and started a riot to fulfil their intention of finally killing Paul.

However, their actions were seen by Roman soldiers in the immediately adjacent fort of Antonia who intervened upon the order of their resident *'chiliarchos'*. This was the Commander of the one thousand soldiers that were based there for the purpose of monitoring and controlling Temple crowd activity, a man subsequently named by Luke as Claudius Lysias.

21:33-36 'Then the commander came up and took hold of him, and ordered him to be bound with two chains; and he began asking who he was and what he had done. But among the crowd some were shouting one thing and some another, and when he could not find out the facts because of the uproar, he ordered him to be brought into the barracks. When he got to the stairs, he was carried by the soldiers because of the violence of the mob; for the multitude of the people kept following them, shouting, "Away with him!"'

Herod the Great had built a palace for himself in the upper part of Jerusalem on the southwestern hill, and had also rebuilt the ancient Hebrew fortress Baris, attaching it to the northeast corner of the newly built Temple, accessed via a broad stone staircase.

Herod added 4 new corner towers and renamed it Antonia in honour of his latest Roman patron Marc Antony (Josephus: 'Antiquities', 15, 8, 1).
.
And so Paul was physically carried by the Roman soldiers through the screaming mob of rioting Jews up the broad staircase into the barracks of fort Antonia.

This would not be the only time Paul would be aided by the Roman army in fulfilling God's plan for his life.

King Herod's development of the existing temple was commenced in 19 BC, but was not completed until 64 AD. Josephus records that the Holy Place was built by one thousand specially trained priests in 18 months (11-10 BC), since the location was in essence a holy building site that only Jewish priests could enter.

The resulting structure was magnificent, resulting in buildings of size and beauty far surpassing anything that had stood there before, or indeed anywhere in the known ancient world.

In 4 BC (the year most commonly assigned to Jesus' birth), there were major civic disturbances following upon the destruction by rabbinic students of the idolatrous Golden Eagle which Herod had erected (contrary to the Jewish Law) over the main gate of the Temple. The history of Herod's Temple is scattered with incidents of similarly violent behaviour, both by Jews and the occupying Roman army which supported the priestly Temple Guard.

The subsequent accession of Herod's son Archelaus was also accompanied by rioting which ended in the death of 3,000 Jews, as a further consequence of his late father's attempt to erect the offensive Golden Eagle.

After this, thinking that order had been restored, Archelaus set out for Rome to have his rulership confirmed by the Emperor. During his absence Sabinus, the incumbent Roman procurator, further disturbed the city's populace, and by the following Passover there had been yet another massacre, this time accompanied by street fighting and open robbery.

Varus, the governor of Syria, who had come to the aid of Sabinus, suppressed this rebellion with ruthless severity and crucified 2,000 more Jews. Archelaus returned from Rome shortly afterward with the rank of ethnarch, an office which he retained until his exile in 6 AD.

During the procuratorship of Pontius Pilate (26-37 AD) there were several disturbances, culminating in a riot consequent upon his taking some of the 'Corban' sacred offerings of the temple for the construction of an aqueduct, enclosing the suburbs, which had grown up north of the second wall and of the temple, by what Josephus calls the 'Third Wall' ('Antiquities', 18,3,2).

In 56AD Herod Agrippa I's son (King) Agrippa, built an addition to the old Hasmonean palace, from which he could overlook the inner Temple area. This act was a major cause of offense to the Jews who in consequence built a wall on the western boundary of the Inner Court to shut off Agrippa's view.

In the resulting quarrel the Jews were successful in gaining the support of Nero. In 64 AD the long rebuilding of the Temple courts, which had been begun in 19 BC, was concluded. The 18,000 ordinary workmen/labourers left unemployed were given temporary work in 'paving the city with white stone', although some may have taken to becoming brigands. (Josephus, 'Antiquities', 15, 8, 1)

The above historical record of religious and social unrest demonstrated the need for Roman law and order. Rome had a particular concern for the safety of its own citizens, and would not hesitate to use their military strength in this regard, as the following chapters of Acts clearly illustrate.

21:37-40 'As Paul was about to be brought into the barracks, he said to the commander,"May I say something to you?" And he said, "Do you know Greek? Then you are not the Egyptian who some time ago stirred up a revolt and led the four thousand men of the Assassins out into the wilderness?" But Paul said, "I am a Jew of Tarsus in Cilicia, a citizen of no insignificant city; and I beg you, allow me to speak to the people." When he had given him permission, Paul, standing on the stairs, motioned to the people with his hand; and when there was a great hush, he spoke to them in the Hebrew dialect, saying:'

Paul clarifies the case of possible mistaken identity that may have led to the Roman army's prompt intervention.

According to Josephus this Egyptian, whose name Luke does not mention, had travelled from Egypt to Jerusalem, said that he was a prophet, and advised the multitude of the common (unlearned) people to go with him to the Mount of Olives. He had said that he would show them how the walls of Jerusalem would fall down; and had promised that he would procure for the Jews a miraculous entrance through the walls when they were to fall down.

Josephus relates, ('Jewish War') that he got together some thirty thousand men that were deceived by him and that 'these he led round from the wilderness to the Mount of Olives, ready to break into Jerusalem by force from that place. But the governor-judge Felix, who had been apprized of his movements, marched against him with the Roman soldiers, and slew four hundred of his followers and took two hundred more as prisoners.'

The shaven headed Apostle, now safely standing high above the crowds of fellow pilgrim Jews, and most probably wearing his Jewish scholar's robes, makes the familiar rabbinic 'quiet please' hand motion and the crowd duly grows silent.

Paul is then able to commence a formal public address in the Hebrew (rabbinic) tongue.

Chapter 22

22:1-2 '"Brethren, and fathers, hear my defence which I now offer to you." And when they heard that he was addressing them in the Hebrew dialect, they became even more quiet; and he said:'

Paul's *'apologia'* (a speech defending/vindicating himself) and delivered in Hebrew, has the effect of further (and now internally) 'calming' the mob that, seconds earlier, had been baying for his blood. 'Even more quiet' is *'hêsuchia'*, which Vine's Dictionary defines as 'tranquility arising from within', i.e. inner calm.

22:3-5 'I am a Jew, born in Tarsus of Cilicia, but brought up in this city, educated under Gamaliel, strictly according to the law of our fathers, being zealous for God just as you all are today. I persecuted this Way to the death, binding and putting both men and women into prisons, as also the high priest and all the Council of the elders can testify. From them I also received letters to the brethren, and started off for Damascus in order to bring even those who were there to Jerusalem as prisoners to be punished.'

Paul would not have immediately been recognised by the mainly pilgrim crowd as a former Sanhedrin associate and so he offers them a glimpse of his personal religious history and scholastic background. This included his recent formal persecutory judicial activities on behalf of the Sanhedrin towards the early Jewish followers of Messiah, now simply designated as 'The Way.' He cites the ruling High Priest Annas and the other seventy ruling elders as witnesses to this, such is his confidence in his own position from a Jewish legal standpoint.

The Greek for 'the brethren' referred to in verse 5, is *'adelphos',* meaning Paul's fellow traditionally orthodox religious Jews, rather than Damascus' relatively new Messianic Jewish refugees. The picture Luke is painting for Caesar's Roman court is persistently one of Paul lacking any straying from the widely established Jewish religious norms. This would go a long way towards ensuring his eventual legal acquittal in Nero's court in Rome.

22:6-11 "'But it happened that as I was on my way, approaching Damascus about noontime, a very bright light suddenly flashed from heaven all around me, and I fell to the ground and heard a voice saying to me, 'Saul, Saul, why are you persecuting me?' And I answered, 'Who are you, Lord?' And he said to me, 'I am Jesus the Nazarene, whom you are persecuting.' And those who were with me saw the light, to be sure, but did not understand the voice of the one who was speaking to me. And I said, 'What shall I do, Lord?' And the Lord said to me, 'Get up and go on into Damascus, and there you will be told of all that has been appointed for you to do.' But since I could not see because of the brightness of that light, I was led by the hand by those who were with me and came into Damascus.'"

Paul recounts the events that occurred on the Damascus Road, emphasising the point that his persecutory behaviour was directed primarily at Jesus himself rather than at his followers, despite the outward appearances to the contrary. Having first got Paul's attention by temporarily blinding him, Jesus would go on to reveal his plans for Paul in incremental stages.

Paul introduces himself to the Temple crowd first of all as a Jew. As he would later write to the congregation at Corinth (2 Corinthians 11:22) and to that at Philippi (Philippians 3:5), this was his defining identity.

He then elaborates further upon his identity as a Roman born citizen from Tarsus. Tarsus was the Roman's major Mediterranean port located at the mouth of the River Cydnus and was the terminus of the great Roman road east through Asia Minor.

It was also one of the greatest university cities of the ancient world. Paul, a highly educated Pharisee, had completed his doctoral training as a Rabbi 'at the feet of Gamaliel' (verse 3), a Doctor of Torah who was known both as a 'Rabban' (the most senior rank of Rabbi) and as 'the glory of the Law.' Gamaliel was the grandson of the great Jewish scholar Hillel, and thought by some scholars to have been the son of the Simeon mentioned as having blessed the infant Jesus in the Temple (recorded in Luke 2:25).

A fanatic for his traditional faith, Saul appears to have sought to surpass his wise teacher and rabbinic master in zeal by becoming a vehement persecutor of many of his fellow Jews out of a misguided passion for his nation's religious ancestral ways.

As he would later write to the Galatians: 'For you have heard of my former manner of life in Judaism, how I used to persecute the church of God beyond, measure and tried to destroy it, and I was advancing in Judaism beyond many of my contemporaries among my countrymen, being more extremely zealous for my ancestral traditions.' (Galatians 1:13-14).

On all of these points Paul was entirely at one with the audience of fanatical religious pilgrim Jews from Asia that moments earlier had been trying to kill him. In the Greek text, to 'the perfect manner of the law' is *'kata akribeian'*, also meaning 'through diligence' and 'to the utmost rigour of instruction'.

'The law of our fathers' refers to the Law which they had received via Moses that which was handed down to the elders (and subsequently to the rabbis). This became the oral Law that was prevalent at the time of Jesus, and which Jesus had set about reforming.

Paul was a Pharisee and considered the rabbinic oral Law to be authoritative and therefore. In describing himself as 'being zealous for God', we are approaching one of the roots of what had surely been driving Paul's extreme persecutory violence. Namely, the deep desire to show himself to be a more fervently religious Jew than even his rabbinic master Gamaliel.

Saul of Tarsus was therefore a highly intelligent Pharisee from a well connected and wealthy Roman-Jewish background, who as an adolescent boy had arrived in

Jerusalem to fulfil the highly regarded role of disciple to the great Rabbi Gamaliel.

From a human behavioral psychological perspective it is highly likely that the foreign (Turkish) born Saul felt that the way he had been raised, as a Jew on spiritually hostile foreign soil, gave him an edge over the older, wiser and milder mannered Gamaliel when it came to religious zeal.

22:12-16 'A certain Ananias, a man who was devout by the standard of the Law, and well spoken of by all the Jews who lived there, came to me, and standing near said to me, 'Brother Saul, receive your sight!' And at that very time I looked up at him. And he said, 'The God of our fathers has appointed you to know his will and to see the Righteous One and to hear an utterance from his mouth. For you will be a witness for him to all men of what you have seen and heard. Now why do you delay? Get up and be baptized, and wash away your sins, calling on his name.'

Accurately, but also with the Roman Court in mind, Luke describes Ananias as a devout, well-regarded Damascene Jew, rather than as a product of a still possibly illegal Messianic splinter-faith group. Ananias is both an instrument of God's healing and a prophetic minister of God's word.

God had chosen Saul to become more aligned to his will and to be guided on this messianic path by being enabled to spiritually see and hear in a new way. This would have the effect of enabling Saul, as indeed all of God's children, to exercise faith, which, as he would later explain to the church in Rome, comes by hearing from God (Romans 10:17).

Saul facilitated this process of spiritual change towards witnessing in the traditional, time-honoured Jewish manner of religious self-immersion, *'baptiseo'*.

It was this further 'witnessing to all men' (including Gentiles) that had done so much to annoy his fellow religious Jews, who regarded themselves as being uniquely special to God. Their reluctance to dilute this inflated sense of self-importance by accommodating Gentiles was a major psychological part of what drove their opposition to Paul's ministry. Jesus had clearly forewarned Paul of their impending negative reaction.

22:17-22 'It happened when I returned to Jerusalem and was praying in the temple, that I fell into a trance, and I saw him saying to me, 'Make haste, and get out of Jerusalem quickly, because they will not accept your testimony about me.' "And I said, "Lord, they themselves understand that in one synagogue after another I used to imprison and beat those who believed in you. And when the blood of your witness Stephen was being shed, I also was standing by approving, and watching out for the coats of those who were slaying him." And he said to me, "Go! For I will send you far away to the Gentiles." They listened to him up to this statement, and then they raised their voices and said, "Away with such a fellow from the earth, for he should not be allowed to live."'

Mentioning the Gentiles once again triggered an extremely hostile response from the previously calmed mob of religious pilgrims. The Jews liked the notion of all non-Jews being spiritually subservient to them.

They regarded the Roman occupation as a major embarrassment to their superior status over Gentiles as keepers of both God's covenant with Abraham and of the law of Moses. The Jews felt that, as the custodians of the Torah, they had a kind of monopoly on God's laws and were blind to the implications of their very recent rejection of One who had the most excellent messianic credentials. They most certainly objected to the idea that the Gentiles could receive God's blessings without first suffering the ignominy and discomfort of adult circumcision, and they expressed their disapproval by shouting, waving their garments and throwing dust in the air.

The manner in which Stephen had so calmly met his execution had clearly impacted Saul deeply. As the Sanhedrin appointed keeper of the outer garments of the official executioners Saul would doubtless have witnessed such violent deaths previously, as he evidently held a formal judicial role in representing the legal enactment of Sanhedrin judgements.

He would have had an excellent view of Stephen's countenance as, looking up in death, Stephen's expression altered to one of angelic brightness (Acts

7:58) as he beheld the risen Jesus standing ready to receive his spirit into heaven's eternal bliss.

A starker contrast with a routine criminal summary execution would be hard to imagine.

Acts 22:23-29 'And as they were crying out and throwing off their cloaks and tossing dust into the air, the commander ordered him to be brought into the barracks, stating that he should be examined by scourging so that he might find out the reason why, they were shouting against him that way. But when they stretched him out with thongs, Paul said to the centurion who was standing by, "Is it lawful for you to scourge a man who is a Roman and uncondemned?" When the centurion heard this, he went to the commander and told him, saying, "What are you about to do? For this man is a Roman." The commander came and said to him, "Tell me, are you a Roman?" And he said, "Yes" The commander answered, "I acquired this citizenship with a large sum of money." And Paul said, "But I was actually born a citizen." Therefore those who were about to examine him immediately let go of him; and the commander also was afraid when he found out that he was a Roman, and because he had put him in chains.'

The commander would not likely have spoken nor understood Hebrew/Aramaic and so did not know what Paul had been saying to the crowd. But he would have been very familiar with Jewish Temple riots and knew he had to deal at once with any man causing one. So he had Paul bound for questioning under scourging, the tried and tested most effective way of extracting truth or a confession.

The Roman scourge was a leather whip studded at intervals with sharp pieces of bone and lead. Few men survived it in their right senses and many died under it.

At this point Paul exercised his rights and privileges as a (legally trained) Roman born citizen.

Cicero is recorded as having said, 'It is a misdeed for a Roman citizen to be bound; it is a crime for him to be beaten; it is almost as bad as to murder a father to kill him.' Roman law expressly forbade binding an unjudged citizen. Livy (4,9) wrote that 'The body of every Roman citizen is inviolable.'

When Paul stated that he was a citizen, the commander was justifiably alarmed. And not only because Paul was a citizen but because he was a free-born citizen, whereas the commander had evidently had to purchase his own freedom as a foreigner who had come under Roman rule as an adult. The commander knew that he had been on the verge of doing something which would have involved certainly his dismissal and not improbably his own execution. So he loosed Paul and determined to confront him with the Sanhedrin in order to get to the bottom of the reason for the Temple riot, while presumably at the same time confirming Paul's claims to citizenship.

22:30 'But on the next day, wishing to know for certain why he had been accused by the Jews, he released him and ordered the chief priests and all the Council to assemble, and brought Paul down and set him before them.'

The ruling Jewish Sanhedrin consisted of 70 men, numbering 23 Sadducees, 23 Pharisees and 23 nobles. The seventieth could be elected as president from either subgroup and they met in the Temple Courts in the 'Hall of Hewn Stones' between the Court of Israel and the Court of the Priests. Saul/Paul had formerly represented the Sanhedrin as a Pharisee of Rabbi Gamaliel's school.

The Roman soldiers took Paul back down the staircase from Antonia and deposited him there, waiting nearby because they now had formal responsibility for his safety as a Roman citizen in their charge.

And so Paul is about to be brought face to face with many of his former colleagues on the Sanhedrin.

Chapter 23

23:1-5 'Paul, looking intently at the Council, said, "Brethren, I have lived my life with a perfectly good conscience before God up to this day." The high priest Ananias commanded those standing beside him to strike him on the mouth. Then Paul said to him, "God is going to strike you, you whitewashed wall! Do you sit to try me according to the Law, and in violation of the Law order me to be struck?" But the bystanders said, "Do you revile God's high priest?" And Paul said, "I was not aware, brethren, that he was high priest; for it is written, 'You shall not speak evil of a ruler of your people.'"

Having undoubtedly spent much of the previous night in prayer, Paul entered the Sanhedrin's meeting hall in the Temple in confidence and faith. 'Looking intently' here is, in the Greek, *atenizô atenizô* .It is translated by Vine's Dictionary as 'to look up steadfastly' and denotes an attitude of undergirding prayerfulness. Paul is remembering Messiah's words as earlier recorded by Luke in his first treatise to Theophilus in Luke 12:12:

12:11-12 "When they bring you before the synagogues and the rulers and the authorities, do not worry about how or what you are to speak in your defence, or what you are to say; for the Holy Spirit will teach you in that very hour what you ought to say."

As Paul gazed heavenwards, he listened to the still, small inner voice of the Holy Spirit, who gave him just the right words to speak.

Lived with a 'perfectly good conscience' is *suneidesis* which in this instance has a particularly Roman connotation. Paul is deliberately reminding the Sanhedrin that he is a Roman citizen and therefore able to avail himself of the protections that his citizenship afforded him. The soldiers that had delivered him to their meeting room were waiting nearby and watching out for him still. He was not simply an ordinary Jew under their supreme authority.

This is taken as an affront to the Sanhedrin's arrogant chairman, the ruling High Priest Ananias, who reacted by ordering that Paul be struck (illegally) for such blatant insolence. The blow brings in turn an indignant response from the Jewish legal scholar, echoing Jesus' words years earlier to his fellow Pharisees.

A 'whitewashed wall' denoted a tomb, so painted to alert Jews to its uncleanness from a religious legal perspective. It was a deliberately offensive remark; aimed at the one whom Paul knew very well to be the current High Priest. At this time in Jewish history, the occupying Romans had taken charge, on political grounds and contrary to Scripture, of appointing the ruling High Priest. This was a state of affairs that the legal scholars of the Pharisees objected to strongly, but were powerless to prevent.

According to Josephus ('Antiquities' 20,5,2) Ananias was the son of Nebedinus and was the ruling High Priest when Quadratus, who preceded Felix as governor, ruled in Syria. He had been sent bound to Rome by Quadratus in 52 AD to answer a charge of cruelty and oppression brought by Samaritans.

The emperor Claudius eventually acquitted him but he was later deposed shortly before Felix left the province. A typically lawless and violent Sadducee, his arrogant and overbearing behaviour described here in Acts is entirely in keeping with the secular Roman historical record.

Given that Paul would have known exactly who he was, both personally and by Ananias' throne and priestly robes, many scholars have debated exactly why Paul would claim to deny this knowledge, especially when he was apparently speaking under the anointing of the Holy Spirit.

Therein lies the answer. The (Jewish) Spirit of God is inspiring in Paul typically Jewish humour - Paul is being deliberately sarcastic. God has a sense of humour - a Jewish one, which frequently utilizes sarcasm. As Psalm 2 says, 'He who sits in the heavens laughs, the Lord scoffs at them.'

When one of the Sanhedrin's bystanders refers to Ananias as 'God's High Priest', Paul's response (effectively, "Oh, I didn't know that he was **God's** High Priest") is similarly a sarcastic reference to the Romans' unlawful manner of appointing Ananias to that role, contrary to Scripture, which clearly stipulated a process of selection involving casting lots (1 Chronicles 2:28, Nehemiah 10:34).

Paul's sarcasm would not have been lost on his former colleagues on the Pharisee side of the Sanhedrin, who would have felt similarly strongly about the Roman interference in their Scripture-based laws about the appointment of the High Priest.

Paul, and indeed God, did not regard the arrogant, corrupt and sinful Ananias as a legitimate High Priest, and his judgment was indeed pending imminently, as Paul stated. Josephus records ('Wars', 2, 17, 18) that, very shortly afterwards, (in 65 AD) the radical Sicarri group of fanatical Jewish religious assassins murdered Ananias, in a typical extremist religious and politically motivated killing.

23:6-8 'But perceiving that one group were Sadducees and the other Pharisees, Paul began crying out in the Council, "Brethren, I am a Pharisee, a son of Pharisees; I am on trial for the hope and resurrection of the dead!" As he said this, there occurred a dissension between the Pharisees and Sadducees, and the assembly was divided. For the Sadducees say that there is no resurrection, nor an angel, nor a spirit, but the Pharisees acknowledge them all.'

After sarcasm comes similarly God-inspired brilliance. It was indeed Jesus' resurrection that had led to Paul's conversion, but the previous day's unrest in the Temple Courts had come from a popular fallacy that Paul appeared to be minimising Torah observance and giving the Gentiles a free pass into the Jews' Old Covenant benefits.

Paul's mention of resurrection promptly split the Sanhedrin and one of their favourite religious arguments duly erupted, fuelled largely by Paul's former Pharisee-aligned colleagues.

23:9 'And there occurred a great uproar; and some of the Scribes of the Pharisaic party stood up and began to argue heatedly, saying, "We find nothing wrong with this man; suppose, a spirit or an angel has spoken to him?"'

Paul's resurrection claim met with particular favour from former associates who served as Scribes on the Council. Scribes were learned/legally trained Scripture copyists who interpreted the Jewish manuscripts and acted as Hebrew religious lawyers. These were Scribes aligned with the Pharisees on the Sanhedrin (therefore more likely to be sympathetic to Paul), whereas other Scribes were Sadducees and acted on behalf of the priests' ruling families.

Their provocative question about angels only served to throw more fuel onto the already extremely heated 'uproar'. The party of the Sadducees denied the existence of angels, and the Scribes' question appears to have been deliberately asked with the intention of inflaming matters further still. The Greek for 'uproar' here is *'kraugê'*, an onomatopoeic word, imitating the raven's cry, also meaning 'clamour' or 'outcry'. The initial ruckus regarding Ananias' legitimacy may well have died down naturally had it not been for this scribal intervention. As it was, their disputing erupted again in an even more heated manner.

23:10 'And as a great dissension was developing, the commander was afraid Paul would be torn to pieces by them and ordered the troops to go down and take him away from them by force, and bring him into the barracks.'

Dissension is *stasis*, also translated as 'insurrection, riot and uproar'. The previous day's riot had been outdoors in the Temple's Court of Israel; this one, in the confines of the Sanhedrin's meeting room, appears to have been every bit as violent, with decades of mutual hatred erupting into one giant brawl between the two bitterly opposed Jewish groups of Sanhedrin rulers.

In fact it appears that Paul himself lent his fellow Pharisee colleagues a hand, perhaps even two. The fact that the Roman soldiers had to use physical 'force' to extract him from the violence indicates a distinct unwillingness on his part to merely spectate!

23:11 'But on the night immediately following, the Lord stood at his side and said, "Take courage; for as you have solemnly witnessed to my cause, at Jerusalem, so you must witness at Rome also."

Paul had previously expressed the desire to visit Rome (Romans 1:10, 15:23). Jesus' nocturnal visit to the fortress Antonia both generally encouraged Paul and specifically endorsed the approach that he'd taken with the Sanhedrin, reconfirming God's intention that Paul testify in similar fashion in the Imperial capital itself.

23:12-15 'When it was day, the Jews formed a conspiracy and bound themselves under an oath, saying that they would neither eat nor drink until they had killed Paul. There were more than forty who formed this plot. They came to the chief priests and the elders and said, "We have bound ourselves under a solemn oath to taste nothing until we have killed Paul. Now therefore, you and the Council notify the commander to bring him down to you, as though you were going to determine his case, by a more thorough investigation; and we for our part are ready to slay him before he comes near the place."'

The 'Jews' in question here are Paul's old adversaries from Asia Minor who had already tried on several occasions to murder Paul without success. This accounts for their 'vow' to fast until they succeeded - if they should fail in their attempt they were scheduled to return to their far off homes shortly anyway, where their bravado and religious oath would not be commonly known.

But with Paul in Roman custody, and the news of his citizenship declaration unlikely yet to be public knowledge, it would have seemed to them to be too good an opportunity to miss. So they enlist the assistance of the Sanhedrin whose senior Priests and Saducean elders would still have been smarting from the recent violence in the Council's meeting room with their (Pharisee) colleagues and with Paul himself.

23:16-22 'But the son of Paul's sister heard of their ambush, and he came and entered the barracks and told Paul. Paul called one of the centurions to him and said, "Lead this young man to the Commander, for he has something to report to him." So he took him and led him to the Commander and said, "Paul the prisoner called me to him and asked me to lead this young man to you since he has something to tell you. The Commander took him by the hand and stepping aside, began to inquire of him privately, "What is it that you have to report to me?" And he said, "The Jews have agreed to ask you to bring Paul down tomorrow to the Council, as though they were going to inquire somewhat more thoroughly about him. "So do not listen to them, for more than forty of them are lying in wait for him who have bound themselves under a curse not to eat or drink until they slay him; and now they are ready and waiting for the promise from you." So the Commander let the young man go, instructing him, "Tell no one that you have notified me of these things."'

Paul is sometimes depicted by Gentile scholars as being a generally socially unremarkable person. Other than his self-evident intelligence and his phenomenal grasp of Hebrew Scripture he is usually reckoned to not be a particularly unusual individual. This passage provides an alternative perspective, as we see his young nephew being given extraordinary VIP treatment in Jerusalem's Roman fort of Antonia.

Not only can this twelve year old boy freely visit a prisoner in Roman custody but the prisoner himself is treated with respectful credibility by the duty Centurion. Furthermore Antonia's Commander also receives the boy extremely deferentially and gives great credence to his message.

So just who was Paul's brother in law? Because this unnamed figure stands behind the boy and was surely very well known to Claudius Lysias who, as the fort's Commander was an extremely important local Roman representative in his own right.

Who paid Theophilus for his legal services? Who paid for Paul's rented Roman house and for the guards assigned to Paul during his two year house arrest? Paul clearly had access to independent financial support - tabernacle making alone would not have been sufficient to begin to cover these costs.

That Paul came from a wealthy Jewish-Roman family is obvious from his being able to have moved from Tarsus to Jerusalem in the first place, to study at 'the feet of Gamaliel' (Acts 22:3). This was not an educational opportunity provided free of charge.

The influence and stature of the boy's father (Paul's brother in law) will soon become abundantly clear.

23:23-24 'And he called to him two of the centurions and said, "Get **two hundred** soldiers ready by the third hour of the night to proceed to Caesarea, with **seventy** horsemen and **two hundred** spearmen." They were also to provide **mounts** to put Paul on and bring him safely to Felix the governor.'

More VIP treatment is evident in Lysias assigning 470 men plus multiple horses to move one prisoner. This is an absolutely extraordinary number relative to the size of Antonia's garrison (1000 men), and cannot begin to be explained by second-hand threats from a few self-starved Jewish pilgrim religious fanatics. Such a huge troop movement would have to be have been personally accounted for to Rome by Lysias as the Jerusalem fort's Commanding Officer.

The only logical explanation lies with the identity of Paul's sister's husband. To elicit such a show of respect from Lysias towards his son, Paul's nephew, and to then assign such a large and disproportionate number of not one but two bodies of Roman infantry (foot soldiers and specialised spearmen) plus seventy cavalry to one prisoner's transfer is certainly a way in which a regional commander might curry favour with another important Roman official, perhaps with a view to obtaining a more prestigious Imperial posting than Jerusalem in the future.

Josephus records numerous contemporary military escorts, yet none larger than fifty soldiers, and that particular escort served to accompany two dignitaries in a time of war. To assign an escort as large as four hundred and seventy men necessitates a stronger reason than simply a single Roman citizen's life being threatened by a relatively few fasting pilgrims. Paul had been officially recognised as a Roman of significance, not simply because of his born a citizen but also because of how important his immediate family was from a Roman social perspective.

23:25-32 'And he wrote a letter having this form: 'Claudius Lysias, to the most excellent governor Felix, greetings. When this man was arrested by the Jews and was about to be slain by them, I came up to them with the troops and rescued him, having learned that he was a Roman. And wanting to ascertain the charge for which they were accusing him, I brought him down to their Council; and I found him to be accused over questions about their Law, but under no accusation deserving death or imprisonment. When I was informed that there would be a plot against the man, I sent him to you at once, also instructing his accusers to bring charges against him before you.'"

Claudius Felix, successor to Cumanus, had been appointed procurator of Judea by the Emperor at the instigation of Jonathan the ruling High Priest at that time (c.58AD).

'Most Excellent' Felix is *'kratistos'*, a Roman title for a judge, the exact same title that Luke had twice addressed Theophilus by, indicating a senior Roman legal figure.

Felix was the brother of Pallas the infamous favorite of Emperor Claudius, and who, according to Tacitus ('Annals' 8, 14), fell into disgrace in 55 AD. Tacitus implies that Felix was joint procurator of Judea, along with Cumanus, before being appointed to the sole command, but Josephus is silent as to this. Both Tacitus and Josephus refer to Felix having succeeded Cumanus in his role as local procurator.

Felix had married three wives in succession, all from royal families, one of whom was Drusilla, who was sister to King Agrippa. Tacitus ('Histories' 5,9) states that 'he governed with all the authority of a king, and the baseness and insolence of a slave'.

On his arrival in Caesarea, sixty miles north of Jerusalem, Paul was presented to Felix and was then detained for five days in the judgment hall of Herod, till his accusers arrived.

The trial began, but after hearing the evidence of Tertullus and the speech of Paul in his own defense, Felix opted to defer judgment.

The excuse Felix gave for delay was the non-appearance of Lysias, but his apparent real reason was in order to attempt to obtain money for the release of Paul. He therefore treated his prisoner at first with leniency and feigned interest in Paul's teaching. Recognising Jewish-Roman family wealth, he attempted to induce Paul to purchase his freedom with bribery.

Uninterested in bribing him, Paul sought the favour of neither Felix nor Drusilla, and made the frequent interviews which he had with them an opportunity for preaching to them concerning righteousness, self-control and the final judgment.

The case dragged on for two years until Felix, upon his retirement, and desiring to gain favour with the Jews, left Paul in prison. This was possibly to also please the Jewish Drusilla as well as the rest of the Judean hierarchy.

Luke's testimony in Acts as to the wicked character of Felix is fully corroborated by the writings of Josephus. Although Felix suppressed the robbers and murderers who infested Judea, including the Egyptian whom Lysias referred to (Acts 21:38), yet 'he himself was more hurtful than them all.' When occasion arose, he did not even hesitate to employ the ultra religious Sicarri-assassins for his own ends.

Trading upon the powerful influence of his brother in Rome, his cruelty and rapacity was great, and during his rule revolts became continuous, marking a distinct stage in the seditious Jewish movement which culminated in the outbreak of war before 70 AD.

23:33-35 'So the soldiers, in accordance with their orders, took Paul and brought him by night to Antipatris. But the next day, leaving the horsemen to go on with him, they returned to the barracks.' When these had come to Caesarea and delivered the letter to the governor, they also presented Paul to him. When he had read it, he asked from what province he was, and when he learned that he was from Cilicia, he said, "I will give you a hearing after your accusers arrive also", giving orders for him to be kept in Herod's Praetorium.'

Antipatris was 25 miles from Caesarea. As far as Antipatris the country was largely inhabited by Jews, but after that was an area largely inhabited by Gentiles which was topographically open and flat, and therefore unsuited for an ambush. At Antipatris the main body of the Roman troops returned to Jerusalem leaving the cavalry to acts as Paul's continuing escort to Caesarea and the delivery of Lysias' letter to Felix.

Herod's Praetorium was the palace that Herod had built for himself in Caesarea and which was later became the civil governor's residence.

Chapter 24

24:1-9 'After five days the high priest Ananias came down with some elders, with an attorney named Tertullus, and they brought charges to the governor against Paul. After Paul had been summoned, Tertullus began to accuse him, saying to the governor, "Since we have through you attained much peace, and since by your providence reforms are being carried out for this nation, we acknowledge this in every way and everywhere, most excellent Felix, with all thankfulness. But, that I may not weary you any further, I beg you to grant us, by your kindness, a brief hearing. For we have found this man a real pest and a fellow who stirs up dissension among all the Jews throughout the world, and a ringleader of the sect of the Nazarenes. And he even tried to desecrate the temple; and then we arrested him. We wanted to judge him according to our own Law. But Lysias the commander came along, and with much violence took him out of our hands, ordering his accusers to come before you. By examining him yourself concerning all these matters you will be able to ascertain the things of which we accuse him."

The Jews also joined in the attack, asserting that these things were so.'

The Temple generated great wealth for Ananias' family, meaning he could certainly afford to hire the best Roman legal counsel, someone who knew how to properly address Felix as the incumbent representative of Roman jurisprudence.

Paul is described as *'loimos'*, a 'plague, pestilence or pest', belonging to the Nazarene 'sect'. This is 'hairesis', meaning 'an opinion' or a heresy. The same term was in regular use of the Pharisees and the Sadducees, and Luke includes it to evidence that the new messianic movement was of a similar nature to these very well established branches of Judaism.

The Temple disturbance is laid firmly at his door; he stirs up *'stasis'* - 'strife and insurrection'. He is described as a 'ringleader' (literally meaning 'one who stood in the first rank') of the *'Nazôraios'*, 'those from Nazareth', an intentionally derogatory term for the early followers of Messiah.

Only in criticising the actions of Lysias did Tertullus possibly err. 'Violent' is *'bia'*, meaning 'military force'. Tertullus also reintroduces the errant allegation of Paul's involvement in Temple desecration, the mistaken view that had helped fuel the indignation of the pilgrim crowds from Asia who had earlier seen Paul in the company of a Greek called Trophimus (Acts 21:29).

He suggests that the Jews were acting lawfully in rioting when Lysias' soldiers had arrived and interfered with their expressing a form of legitimate religious righteous indignation.

24:10-15 'When the governor had nodded for him to speak, Paul responded: "Knowing that for many years you have been a judge to this nation, I cheerfully make my defence, since you can take note of the fact that no more than twelve days ago I went up to Jerusalem to worship. Neither in the temple, nor in the synagogues, nor in the city itself did they find me carrying on a discussion with anyone or causing a riot, Nor can they prove to you the charges of which they now accuse me. But this I admit to you, that according to the Way which they call a sect I do serve the God of our fathers, believing everything that is in accordance with the Law and that is written in the Prophets; having a hope in God, which these men cherish themselves, that there shall certainly be a resurrection of both the righteous and the wicked.'"

Paul was himself legally qualified (in Jewish law) and was quite undisturbed by Tertullus' allegations, pointing out to Felix that there was plenty of independent testimony as to the events in the Temple on the day of his arrest and that he himself had not been party to causing any disturbance whatsoever. Consequently none of the Jewish leaders' allegations could be proved, they were producing no eye witnesses and in fact the instigators of both the complaints in general and of the riot in particular were absent (verse 19), being by that time presumably back home in Asia Minor.

Having evidenced his adversaries' complete non-case, Paul takes the golden opportunity afforded him to recount the Scriptural promises of the God he served. He points out that both he (a Pharisee) and his priestly adversaries share a common belief, namely a coming judgment that will separate eternally those right with God from the wicked and unrighteous. The adulterous

Felix would have been in no doubt as to which of these two categories he personally fell into from the Jewish religious perspective.

24:16-21 "'In view of this, I also do my best to maintain always, a blameless conscience both before God and before men. Now after several years I came to bring alms to my nation and to present offerings; in which they found me occupied in the temple, having been purified, without, any crowd or uproar. But there were some Jews from Asia, who ought to have been present before you and to make accusation, if they should have anything against me. Or else let these men themselves tell what misdeed they found when I stood before the Council, other than for this one statement which I shouted out while standing among them, 'For the resurrection of the dead I am on trial before you today.'"

Paul cleverly repeats his point about his 'good conscience' - *suneidêsis*, the same Roman-friendly term that had so upset Ananias a few days earlier in the Sanhedrin's chamber in the Temple. Having already declared himself to be a good Jew, Paul once again declares himself to be a good Roman citizen, one who, unlike Ananias and company, happens to believe in bodily resurrection.

24:22-23 'But Felix, having a more exact knowledge about the Way, put them off, saying, "When Lysias the commander comes down, I will decide your case." Then he gave orders to the centurion for him to be kept in custody and yet have some freedom, and not to prevent any of his friends from ministering to him.'

Felix clearly recognised Paul's elevated standing as a Roman, granting him special privileges. Felix was at that time married to Drusilla, a Jewess. She would certainly have heard about Paul's fellow Temple scholar Jesus of Nazareth, not least for the revolutionary way in which, contrary to rabbinic practice and indeed Roman custom, he treated women as equal with men in their relations toward God, teaching and discipling them both publically and in private.

Jesus had been a well-known rabbinic teacher in addition to having had Temple construction connections via his father Joseph, and Felix clearly knew of him and his messianic claims. Additionally, Drusilla would doubtless have informed Felix of what the followers of 'The Way' were likewise preaching, hence Luke's reference to Felix's 'more exact knowledge'. The Greek text for 'exact' is *'akribos'*, also meaning 'accurate' and 'thorough'. Jesus had been a very well known and extremely popular teacher, with support from prominent leading Roman women in particular, something that Luke had already extensively written to Theophilus about in his earlier treatise. (Luke 8:3).

Drusilla was the daughter of Herod Agrippa the elder, and had been engaged to be married to Epiphanes, the son of King Antiochus, on condition that he would embrace the Jewish religion; but because he afterwards refused to do that, their marriage contract was broken off.

After that she was given in marriage, by her brother Agrippa the younger, to Azizus king of Emesa, conditional upon his consent to be circumcised.

When Felix was governor of Judea, he saw Drusilla, fell in love with her and sent to her one of his friends, a Cyprian Jew named Atomos, who, by pretending to be a magician, persuaded her to forsake her husband, and to marry Felix instead. Accordingly, in order to avoid the envy of her sister Bernice, who treated her poorly out of envy of her great beauty. Josephus ('Antiquities' 20,7, 1-2) also records that she was prevailed upon to transgress the Jewish Law and to (illegally) marry Felix.

She was notorious, therefore, for technically living in adultery with him, a scandalous situation amongst Jews. This was almost certainly the reason why Paul emphasized 'self-control' and 'the coming judgment' in his discourse before Felix, thereby demonstrating an initiative that was as bold as it was biblical.

24:24-27 'But some days later Felix arrived with Drusilla, his wife who was a Jewess, and sent for Paul and heard him speak about faith in Christ Jesus. But as he was discussing righteousness, self-control and the judgment to come, Felix became frightened and said, "Go away for the present, and when I find time I will summon you." At the same time too, he was hoping that money would be given him by Paul; therefore he a used to send for him quite often and converse with him. But after two years had passed, Felix was succeeded by Porcius Festus, and wishing to do the Jews a favour, Felix left Paul imprisoned.'

Once again, Paul took advantage of the extraordinary privilege his arrest had afforded him, the opportunity to effectively preach to leading Romans. On this occasion he targeted his message at Felix's rather unlawful marital circumstances. Felix's 'frightened' reaction is evidence that Paul's words were finding their mark.

The unstable Felix then went too far once too often and got recalled to Rome. There was a longstanding argument as to whether Caesarea was a Jewish or a Greek city and Jews and Greeks were at odds over this. There happened to be an outbreak of mob violence in which the Jews came off best, prompting Felix to dispatch his troops to aid the Gentile Greeks. Thousands of Jews were killed and the troops, with Felix's consent and encouragement, sacked and looted the houses of the wealthiest Jews in the city.

Accordingly the Jews did what all Roman provincials had a right to do, which was to report their governor to Rome. That was why Felix left Paul in prison, even though he was well aware that Paul should have been liberated. Felix was trying to curry favour with the Jews' priestly leadership, which didn't do him any good. He was dismissed from his governorship and it was only the personal influence of his brother Pallas (formerly the infamous favorite of Emperor Claudius) that saved him from being executed.

The Emperor Nero then appointed Fe formalstus as Felix's successor. Josephus relates: Josephus

('Antiquities' 20, 8,9) relates that 'When Porcine Festus was sent as successor to Felix by Nero, the principal inhabitants of Caesarea went up to Rome to accuse Felix; and he would certainly have been brought to punishment, unless Nero had yielded to the importunate solicitations of his brother Pallas, who was at that time had in the greatest honour by him.'

Chapter 25

25:1-5 'Festus then, having arrived in the province, three days later went up to Jerusalem from Caesarea. And the chief priests and the leading men of the Jews brought charges against Paul, and they were urging him, requesting a concession against Paul, that he might have him brought to Jerusalem (at the same time, setting an ambush to kill him on the way). Festus then answered that Paul was being kept in custody at Caesarea and that he himself was about to leave shortly. "Therefore," he said. "let the influential men among you go there with me, and if there is anything wrong about the man, let them prosecute him."'

Festus was a very different type of judge to Felix. Unlike Felix, he served his term of office as judge without serious incident.

On arrival in the region, he met in Jerusalem with the latest Roman appointed High Priest (this now being Ismael, the son of Fabi, who had been promoted to that office by King Agrippa) together with his chief priests and those others on the Sanhedrin still leading the Jews' efforts to end Paul's life.

Festus deftly bats away their urgency, referring them to Caesarea for a Roman formal legal hearing.

25:6-8 'After he had spent not more than eight or ten days among them, he went down to Caesarea, and on the next day he took his seat on the tribunal and ordered Paul to be brought. After Paul arrived, the Jews who had come down from Jerusalem stood around him, bringing many and serious charges against him which they could not prove, while Paul said in his own defence, "I have committed no offense either against the Law of the Jews or against the temple or against Caesar."

Being factually completely baseless, the Sanhedrin members present are unable to evidence their charges. Luke emphasises this important point for the benefit of Caesar's Court in Rome, to which Paul is about to exercise his right of appeal to as any citizen could.

25:9-12 'But Festus, wishing to do the Jews a favour, answered Paul and said, "Are you willing to go up to Jerusalem and stand trial before me on these charges?" But Paul said, "I am standing before Caesar's tribunal, where I ought to be tried. I have done no wrong to the Jews, as you also very well know. "If, then, I am a wrongdoer and have committed anything worthy of death, I do not refuse to die; but if none of those things is true of which these men accuse me, no one can hand me over to them. I appeal to Caesar." Then when Festus had conferred with his council, he answered, "You have appealed to Caesar, to Caesar you shall go."'

Festus was well aware of the issues his predecessor Felix had had with the Jews, so he offers Paul a kind of compromise - have a trial in Jerusalem, but before his judgment seat, rather than before the Sanhedrin. This would give the Jews the opportunity to assassinate Paul en route, a possibility Festus appears not to be considering, or, alternatively, is well aware of such that he makes the offer anticipating that Paul will refuse it.

Paul is all too well aware of the danger he is in and so, protesting his innocence, plays his trump card of a citizen's appeal to the Emperor. This left Festus with no legal option other than to fulfil Jesus' words to Paul concerning his testifying in Rome.

In appealing to Caesar, Paul was exercising his legal rights of Roman citizenship. The Roman Valerian, Porcian and Sempronian laws decreed that if any magistrate should be about to beat or threaten with death any Roman citizen, then the accused could appeal to the Roman people and such an appeal automatically carried their case to Rome. The law had been adapted under various emperors, such that any citizen's case could be brought before the Emperor's Court instead of before the people.

All citizens had this right of judicial appeal; and when it was made, the accused had to be sent to Rome for trial. Thus Pliny (Ep. 10, 97) states that those Christians who were accused, and were Roman citizens, appealed to Caesar and were sent to Rome to be tried.

The reasons Paul made this appeal were that he saw that not only would Roman justice probably not be done him by the new governor Festus, but also that his life would be once again endangered by being transferred back to Jerusalem. He had been tried by Felix, and justice had been denied him; and he was now being detained as a prisoner in violation of Roman law and without proper charges having been brought against him, simply to gratify the vengeful Sanhedrin leadership.

It was in this way that Paul's long-cherished desire to see the Roman church, and to preach the gospel there (Romans 1:9-11) was to be fulfilled.

He had already written to the infant church there, assuring them of his intention to 'impart a **gift to strengthen them**, that they might be **mutually encouraged** in their faith.' In writing this it was highly unlikely that Paul had envisioned arriving in Rome as a prisoner in chains, awaiting trial.

This is yet another example of God's sense of humour. Paul would not have foreseen his intention of making a gift of 'strength' being played out through his arriving in Rome in chains.

25:13-16 'Now when several days had elapsed, King Agrippa and Bernice arrived at Caesarea and paid their respects to Festus. While they were spending many days there, Festus laid Paul's case, before the king, saying, "There is a man who was left as a prisoner by Felix; and when I was at Jerusalem, the chief priests and the elders of the Jews brought charges against him, asking for a sentence of condemnation against him. I answered them that it is not the custom of the Romans to hand over any man before the accused meets his accusers face to face and has an opportunity to make his defence against the charges."

King Agrippa (Agrippa II) was the son of Herod Agrippa (Acts 12:1) and a great grandson of Herod the Great. His mother was Cypros (Josephus' 'Wars' 2,9,6).

When his father Herod Agrippa I died, Agrippa II was living in Rome and was a friend of the emperor Claudius. Josephus says that the emperor was inclined to bestow upon him all his father s dominions, but was dissuaded by his ministers. The reason of this was that it was thought imprudent to bestow so large a kingdom on so young a man, and one very inexperienced. Accordingly, Claudius initially sent Cuspius Fadus to be the procurator of Judea (Josephus' 'Antiquities' 19,9,2). Claudius later also bestowed on him the tetrarchy of Philip and Batanea, and then added Trachonitis with Abila (Josephus' 'Antiquities' 20, 7, 1).

After the death of Claudius, Nero (his successor) further added to King Agrippa's dominions parts of Perea and of Galilee too, thereby bringing his rule to a scale on a par with his famous grandfather, Herod the Great.

Like many of the descendants of the Roman's client kings, Agrippa II had been educated from childhood in Rome and was therefore strongly attached to the Roman hierarchy.

When the war commenced in Judea which ended in the destruction of Jerusalem in AD 70, Agrippa did all that he could to preserve peace and order, but in vain.

He afterwards joined his troops with those of the Romans, and assisted them at the destruction of Jerusalem. After the capture of that city, he went back to Rome with his half-sister Bernice, where he died at the age of seventy years, c. A.D. 90.

This manner of living as husband to his half-sister gave cause to great scandal and reproach from the local Jewish populace. Bernice was the eldest daughter of Herod Agrippa I (Acts 12) who had ruled from 38-45 AD.

Bernice was sister to Felix's wife Drusilla and her whole life was incestuous, being described by both Josephus (Antiquities, 19, 5, 1) and Juvenal (6,156). Her first husband was her own uncle, Herod of Chalcis.

Later she married King Ptolemy of Sicily, who for her sake embraced Judaism, by becoming circumcised.

Later on she figured shamefully in the lives of the Roman generals Vespasian and Titus, (father and son) trading on her royal standing to survive the Roman-Jewish war AD 6565-70.

25:17-22 'So after they had assembled here, I did not delay, but on the next day took my seat on the tribunal and ordered the man to be brought before me. When the accusers stood up, they began bringing charges against him not of such crimes as I was expecting, but they simply had some points of disagreement with him about their own religion and about a dead man, Jesus, whom Paul asserted to be alive. Being at a loss how to investigate such matters, I asked whether he was willing to go to Jerusalem and there stand trial on these matters. But when Paul appealed to be held in custody for the Emperor's decision, I ordered him to be kept in custody until I send him to Caesar. Then Agrippa said to Festus, "I also would like to hear the man myself" "Tomorrow," he said, you shall hear him."'

At this time Nero was the reigning Emperor. He had insisted that the title 'Lord', previously dropped by Augustus and Tiberius, be reinstated and applied to him.

Festus found himself in the difficult position of having a Roman citizen who, involved in a Jewish religious dispute, had appealed to Caesar but who had yet to be charged with any offence whatsoever against Roman law.

Furthermore the prisoner was evidently wealthy and from a notable Jewish-Roman family who were unlikely to tolerate an indefinite period of imprisonment without any charges being brought - it was indeed 'absurd' - verse 27.

And so Festus sought the advice of the premier local Jewish Romans - Agrippa and Bernice, Herodian nobility, but not exactly from Judean religious society's top moral drawer. God would use the encounter to communicate his word to the most notorious couple in the region.

25:23-27 'So, on the next day when Agrippa came together with Bernice amid great pomp, and entered the auditorium accompanied by the commanders and the prominent men of the city, at the command of Festus, Paul was brought in. Festus said , "King Agrippa, and all you gentlemen here present with us, you see this man about whom all the people of the Jews appealed to me, both at Jerusalem and here, loudly declaring that he ought not to live any longer. But I found that he had committed nothing worthy of death; and since he himself appealed to the Emperor, I decided to send him. Yet I have nothing definite about him to write to my lord. Therefore I have brought him before you all and especially before you, King Agrippa, so that after the investigation has taken place, I may have something to write. For it seems absurd to me in sending a prisoner, not to indicate also the charges against him."'

And so one of the most notorious sinners came with her half-brother/husband to hear the gospel from the great Jewish scholar and Apostle himself.

Luke is at pains to record the local procurator's words "he has committed nothing worthy of death", a statement that would eventually carry enormous weight in the Court of Nero in Rome, possibly even guaranteeing Paul's eventual acquittal.

Chapter 26

26:1-3 'Agrippa said to Paul, "You are permitted to speak for yourself." Then Paul stretched out his hand and proceeded to make his defence:

"In regard to all the things of which I am accused by the Jews, I consider myself fortunate, King Agrippa, that I am about to make my defence before you today; especially because you are an expert in all customs and questions among the Jews; therefore I beg you to listen to me patiently."'

And so the legally trained and righteous Jewish Torah scholar defends his religious position and delivers God's word to the Roman educated adulterous Herodian, seated next to his beautiful but incestuous wife/half-sister in Festus' Court. One can only marvel at the glorious irony of this when viewed from the perspective of heaven's throne room.

It may appear to first glance that Paul is flattering Agrippa, but actually he is, in typical rabbinic manner, exercising a rather sarcastic sense of humour. Jewish 'customs' certainly encompassed marriage and especially incest.

'Questions' is *'zêtêma'* - 'controversies', and Agrippa would have been in no doubt as what this Pharisaic scholar was obliquely referring to. It is no wonder that Paul asks for his patience.

26:4-8 'So then, all Jews know my manner of life from my youth up, which from the beginning was spent among my own nation and at Jerusalem; since they have known about me for a long time, if they are willing to testify, that I lived as a Pharisee according to the strictest sect of our religion. And now I am standing trial for the hope of the promise made by God to our fathers; the promise to which our twelve tribes hope to attain, as they earnestly, serve God night and day. And for this hope, O King, I am being accused by Jews. Why is it considered incredible among you people if God does raise the dead?'"

The incestuous 'elephant in the room' is highlighted by Paul's direct comparison with his own manner of life, one evidently just as well known for its piety as Agrippa and Bernice's were known for their flagrantly irreligious immorality. Paul, like them, is known 'to all the Jews', both at home in Roman Cilicia and now also in Jerusalem, through his discipleship to Rabbi Gamaliel and his official services to the Sanhedrin.

Pharisees were noted for their belief in resurrection - it was hardly an obscure fringe religious view. 'The hope of the promise made by God' refers to the long awaited Messiah. Mainstream Judaism then (and today) focussed on the triumphant king aspect of their Hebrew Scripture's prophetic writings, sadly overlooking the passages referencing a suffering servant.

Paul has discovered that Messiah Jesus' apparently inglorious death was also for the Gentiles' benefit, a step too far for the majority of his Temple contemporaries.

26:9-11 "'So then, I thought to myself that I had to do many things hostile to the name of Jesus of Nazareth. And this is just what I did in Jerusalem; not only, did I lock up many of the saints in prisons, having received authority from the chief priests, but also when they were being put to death I cast my vote against them. And as I punished them often in all the synagogues, I tried to force them to blaspheme; and being furiously enraged at them, I kept pursuing them even to foreign cities.'"

In these verses we can see what was at the heart of Saul/Paul's initial violent rejection of Jesus' ministry. Paul had been a Temple school contemporary of Jesus', overlapping with him in the seventeen years it took to graduate from the rabbinic academy in Bet Midrash. This is where Luke (in chapter 3 of his Gospel treatise) has already portrayed the twelve year old boy Jesus so amazing the resident Doctors of Torah on a earlier family Passover visit.

Saul had a superb level of expertise in handling both the Hebrew Scriptures and particularly the Law of Moses. When Jesus began to make both direct and indirect claims of divinity, Paul, like most religious Jews, felt that his idol had developed feet of clay. Adulation gave way to an overwhelming sense of spiritual betrayal, one that overflowed into a madness of uncontrollable rage.

Betrayal is one of the most powerful psychological drivers of extreme human behaviour. Paul tells Agrippa that he was 'furiously enraged.' The Greek here is *'perissôs emmainomai '*, literally meaning 'abundantly maddened to the point of raving'.

The shock of Jesus apparently breaking the Jews' central laws of blasphemy had evidently driven Saul/Paul temporarily insane, expressed in his murdering of Jesus' disciples, as far as his devolved Sanhedrin legal authority allowed him to.

A brilliant student of rabbinic law and the Hebrew Scripture in his own right, Saul would naturally also have been earlier in great awe of Jesus' breathtaking supernatural grasp of both Scripture and Torah, just as the Doctors of the Law had been years earlier.

26:12-18 "'While so engaged as I was journeying to Damascus with the authority and commission of the chief priests, at midday, O King, I saw on the way a light from heaven, brighter than the sun, shining all around me and those who were journeying with me. And when we had all fallen to the ground, I heard a voice saying to me in the Hebrew dialect, `Saul, Saul, why are you persecuting me? It is hard for you to kick against the goads.' And I said, `Who are you, Lord?' And the Lord said, `I am Jesus whom you are persecuting. But get up and stand on your feet; for this purpose I have appeared to you, to appoint you a minister and a witness not only to the things which you have seen , but also to the things in which I will appear to you; rescuing you from the Jewish people and from the Gentiles, to whom I am sending you, to open their eyes so that they may turn from darkness to light and from the dominion of Satan to God, that they may receive forgiveness of sins and an inheritance among those who have been sanctified by faith in me.'"

Paul repeats his description of meeting the risen Lord Jesus on the Damascus Road. He gives an account of his marching orders, namely to be a 'minister' and a 'witness' of Messiah to both Jew and Gentile.

'Minister' is a rather weak translation of *'hupêretês'*, a well known term meaning an 'under-rower'. The era's large Roman navy's ships were mainly powered utilising lower deck slaves chained to oars and obeying orders from the deck above them. This is an excellent image of true Christian ministry, emphasising genuine hiddenness of service and a complete absence of the egotism commonly associated with modern-day celebrity Christianity.

True believers should row harmoniously to the rhythm set by the upper deck's Heavenly Captain, confident that his hand is on the tiller and that his eyes miss nothing, no matter how dark the circumstances may appear to be.

'Witness' is, of course, *'martus'* - 'martyr'- and very often physical death was indeed the outcome, however, a response of faith would secure both forgiveness of sins and an 'inheritance' (*'klêros'* - 'a portion') in Messiah's kingdom.

26:19-23 '"So, King Agrippa, I did not prove disobedient to the heavenly vision, but kept declaring both to those of Damascus first, and also at Jerusalem and then throughout all the region of Judea, and even to the Gentiles, that they should repent and turn to God, performing deeds appropriate to repentance. For this reason some Jews seized me in the temple and tried to put me to death. So, having obtained help from God, I stand to this day testifying both to small and great, stating nothing but what the Prophets and Moses said was going to take place; that the Christ was to suffer, and that by reason of his resurrection from the dead he would be the first to proclaim light both to the Jewish people and to the Gentiles."'

Paul, despite being in chains, is very much in command of the hearing, and now brings the spotlight back onto King Agrippa, for whom repentance and turning to God were pertinent themes indeed.

Paul was simply obeying the directions of Moses and the Prophets, both of which he knew Agrippa firmly believed in. The risen Messiah was shining his spiritual light, but how would Agrippa respond?

It was Paul's mission to the Gentiles that had offended the Jews both in Asia Minor and in Jerusalem, in part out of their pride and in part because they considered Jesus to have been an accursed blasphemer. Would Agrippa fall into the same errors?

26:24-29 'While Paul was saying this in his defence, Festus said in a loud voice, "Paul, you are out of your mind! Your great learning is driving you mad." But Paul said, I am not out of my mind, most excellent Festus, but I utter words of sober truth. "For the king knows about these matters, and I speak to him also with confidence, since I am persuaded that none, of these things escape his notice; for this has not been done in a corner. "King Agrippa, do you believe the Prophets? I know that you do." Agrippa replied to Paul, "In a short time you will persuade me to become a Christian." And Paul said, "I would wish to God, that whether in a short or long time, not only you, but also all who hear me this day, might become such as I am, except for these chains.'"

Paul presented his case for Messiah's credibility so well that King Agrippa is almost persuaded to believe.

Festus' outburst concerning Paul's 'great learning' was almost certainly born from a sense of embarrassment for his royal guests' personal feelings.

26:30-32 'The king stood up and the governor and Bernice, and those who were sitting with them, and when they had gone aside, they began talking to one another, saying, "This man is not doing anything worthy of death or imprisonment." And Agrippa said to Festus, "This man might have been set free if he had not appealed to Caesar."

Agrippa's comments regarding Paul's innocence, recorded by Luke, would go a long way towards securing Paul's eventual acquittal in Rome. The text does not record what assistance, if any, Festus received in documenting Roman legal charges against Paul.

Perhaps 'various unproven Jewish allegations and complaints' sufficed….

Chapter 27

27:1-4 'When it was decided that we would sail for Italy, they proceeded to deliver Paul and some other prisoners to a Centurion of the Augustan cohort named Julius. And embarking in an Adramyttian ship, which was about to sail to the regions along the coast of Asia, we put out to sea accompanied, by Aristarchus, a Macedonian of Thessalonica. The next day we put in at Sidon; and Julius treated Paul with consideration and allowed him to go to his friends and receive care. From there we put out to sea and sailed under the shelter of Cyprus because the winds were contrary.'

'We would sail' indicates that Luke accompanied Paul on what was probably a locally operated merchant ship as opposed to an official Roman navy vessel. The faithful Thessalonian Aristarchus also accompanied Paul, as he would continue to in the future, even as far as a later Roman imprisonment (Colossians 4:10). The ship was embarking from Andramyttium, a port town on the Roman road between Troas and Ephesus. Sea journeys between Caesarea and Rome usually involved at least one change of craft en route.

According to both Tacitus and Suetonius ('Annals' 14, 15, and 'Life of Nero' 20), the current Emperor (Nero), had instituted an Imperial bodyguard of 4-600 men consisting of Sabastene ('Augustani') cavalry from Rome's' Equestrian order, supported by foot soldiers. These soldiers could well have accompanied Festus on his journey out from Rome, and if so, would now be returning to Rome. Considering Paul's family's social background, education, etc, it is not surprising that their Centurion Julius treated Paul well.

The sea journey continued along the coast as far as Sidon, 67 miles north of Caesarea, where Paul received support from local believers. From there they crossed below Cyprus to avoid an opposing westerly headwind common at that late time of year ('The Fast' being the Day of Atonement, which occurred in October).

27:5-8 'When we had sailed through the sea along the coast of Cilicia and Pamphylia, we landed at Myra in Lycia. There the centurion found an Alexandrian ship sailing for Italy, and he put us aboard it. When we had sailed slowly for a good many days, and with difficulty had arrived off Cnidus, since the wind did not permit us to go farther, we sailed under the shelter of Crete, off Salmone; and with difficulty sailing past it we came to a place called Fair Havens, near which was the city of Lasea'.

Myra in Lycia (southwest Asia Minor) was a common destination for the Egyptian ships that exported grain to the markets in Rome.

27:9-13 'When considerable time had passed and the voyage was now dangerous, since even the fast was already over, Paul began to admonish them, and said to them, "Men, I perceive that the voyage will certainly be with damage and great loss, not only of the cargo and the ship, but also of our lives." But the Centurion was more persuaded by the pilot and the Captain of the ship than by what was being said by Paul. Because the harbour was not suitable for wintering, the majority reached a decision to put out to sea from there, if somehow they could reach Phoenix, a harbour of Crete, facing southwest and northwest, and spend the winter there. When a moderate south wind came up, supposing that they had attained their purpose, they weighed anchor and *began* sailing along Crete, close inshore.'

Paul was an experienced traveller and knew that such sailings were generally considered risky after September and very difficult by November. Ancient ships had neither sextant nor compass and in cloudy and dark weather they had no means of checking their course. So Paul's wise advice was that they should winter in Fair Havens where they were. The ship was an Alexandrian corn ship; the 'owner' was therefore a corn dealer who was bringing the cargo of corn across to the bread markets in Rome.

The Centurion, as the senior officer on board, had the final say in the decision, although it is significant that Paul, a prisoner, was allowed to give his input when counsel was being taken, another indicator of his high standing both as a well known Jewish Temple scholar and as a naturally born Roman citizen.

Fair Havens was not considered a very good harbour nor was it near any sizeable town where the winter days might be passed by the crew; so the Centurion rejected Paul's advice and instead took the advice of the ship's master and the corn contractor to sail farther along the coast to Phoenix where there was a larger harbour and associated town.

27:14-20 'But before very long there rushed down from the land a violent wind, called Euraquilo ; and when the ship was caught in it and could not face the wind, we gave way to it and let ourselves be driven along. Running under the shelter of a small island called Clauda, we were scarcely able to get the ship's boat under control. After they had hoisted it up, they used supporting cables in undergirding the ship; and fearing that they might run aground on the shallows of Syrtis, they let down the sea anchor and in this way let themselves be driven along. The next day as we were being violently storm-tossed, they began to jettison the cargo; and on the third day they threw the ship's tackle overboard with their own hands. Since neither sun nor stars appeared for many days, and no small storm was assailing us, from then on all hope of our being saved was gradually abandoned.'

An unexpected south wind initially made their reasoning seem correct but then they were struck by a strong north-east gale. 'Euraquilo' means 'violent agitation', from *euros'* - 'east wind'.

The peril was that if they could not control the ship they would inevitably be blown onto the 'Syrtis Sands' off the North African coast which had been the graveyard of many Mediterranean vessels.

The crew had managed to get the ship's dinghy, which had been towed behind, on board, to prevent it either becoming water-logged or dashed to pieces against the ship. They then began to throw out all the ship's surplus gear in order to lighten it. With the stars and the sun shut out by the darkness of the storm, they did not know where they were and the terror of the Syrtis Sands gripped them to such an extent that they abandoned hope of surviving.

Egyptian corn ships were very large vessels, up to 140 feet long and 36 feet wide and of 33 feet draught. In a storm they had certain disadvantages. They had no rudder but were steered with two paddles from the stern on each side. They were consequentially very difficult to manage, being equipped with only one mast, a large square of linen augmented with stitched leather skins. The ship therefore could not be sailed directly into the wind, and this placed great strain on the ship's timbers in a gale such that often they started to separate causing the ship to founder and sink. It was to avoid this danger that the crew passed rope hawsers under the ship and drew them tight with winches to hold the ship together.

27:21-26 'When they had gone a long time without food, then Paul stood up in their midst and said, "Men, you ought to have followed my advice and not to have set sail from Crete and incurred this damage and loss. Yet now I urge you to keep up your courage, for there will be no loss of life among you, but only of the ship. For this very night an angel of the God to whom I belong and whom I serve stood before me, saying, 'Do not be afraid, Paul; you must stand before Caesar; and behold, God has granted you all those who are sailing with you. Therefore, keep up your courage, men, for I believe God that it will turn out exactly, as I have been told. But we must run aground on a certain island."'

At this critical point in the journey Paul's leadership again came to the fore, despite his being a prisoner, fortified spiritually by the timely arrival of a messenger-angel the previous night, presumably during the apostle's time of prayer. Faith comes from the act of hearing a word from God (Romans 10:17), and Paul's resultant confidence served to boost the flagging morale of his fellow travellers.

27:27-32 'But when the fourteenth night came, as we were being driven about in the Adriatic Sea, about midnight, the sailors began to surmise that they were approaching some land. They took soundings and found it to be twenty fathoms; and a little farther on they took another sounding and found it to be fifteen fathoms. Fearing that we might run aground somewhere on the rocks, they cast four anchors from the stern and wished for daybreak. But as the sailors were trying to escape from the ship and had let down the ship's boat into the sea, on the pretence of intending to lay out anchors from the bow, Paul said to the centurion and to the soldiers, "Unless, these men remain in the ship, you yourselves cannot, be saved." Then the soldiers cut away the ropes of the ship's boat and let it fall away.'

The 'Adriatic Sea' lay around the island of Malta between Greece, Italy, and Africa. Fathoms were six foot (depth) measurements derived as the distance between the tips of the middle fingers with the arms stretched wide apart.

Ships were slowed down using anchors lowered from the rear, which the crew pretended to do, intending to escape from the storm in the ships dinghy, until the alert apostle intervened, saving lives by once again demonstrating his observational and leadership skills.

27:33-38 'Until the day was about to dawn, Paul was encouraging them all to take some food, saying, Today is the fourteenth day that you have been constantly watching and going without eating, having taken nothing. Therefore I encourage you to take some food, for this is for your preservation, for not a hair from the head of any of you will perish. Having said this, he took bread and gave thanks to God in the presence of all, and he broke it and began to eat. All of them were encouraged and they themselves also took food. All of us in the ship were two hundred and seventy-six persons. When they had eaten enough, they began to further lighten the ship by throwing out the wheat into the sea.'

More leadership was shown with Paul calmly reassuring and persuading his fellow travellers to strengthen themselves with food, preparatory to the physical work involved in jettisoning their cargo in order to raise the ship's level in the sea by lightening the load that it was carrying.

27:39-44 'When day came, they could not recognize the land; but they did observe a bay with a beach, and they resolved to drive the ship onto it if they could. And casting off the anchors, they left them in the sea while at the same time they were loosening the ropes of the rudders; and hoisting the foresail to the wind, they were heading for the beach. But striking a reef where two seas met, they ran the vessel aground; and the prow stuck fast and remained immovable, but the stern began to be broken up by the force of the waves. The soldiers' plan was to kill the prisoners, so that none of them would swim away and escape; but the centurion, wanting to bring Paul safely through, kept them from their intention, and commanded that those who could swim should jump overboard first and get to land, and the rest should follow, some, on planks, and others, on various things from the ship. And so it happened that they all were brought safely to land.'

The morning light enabled the crew to identify a bay that appeared potentially suitable for grounding the ship upon. Unfortunately they hit a submerged sandbank causing the vessel's progress to abruptly halt, while the waves continued to pound at the stern.

The Roman soldiers were naturally concerned with the possibility of their prisoners escaping in the ensuing chaos, an eventuality which they would be obliged, under Roman law, to pay for with their own lives.

Julius' personal intervention saved Paul as well as the others - a further tribute to the high regard that the apostle was so evidently held in.

Chapter 28

28:1-6 'When they had been brought safely through, then we found out that the island was called Malta. The natives showed us extraordinary kindness; for because of the rain that had set in and because of the cold, they kindled a fire and received us all. But when Paul had gathered a bundle of sticks and laid them on the fire, a viper came out because of the heat and fastened itself on his hand. When the natives saw the creature hanging from his hand, they began saying to one another, "Undoubtedly this man is a murderer, and though he has been saved from the sea, justice has not allowed him to live." However, he shook the creature off into the fire and suffered no harm. But they were expecting that he was about to swell up or suddenly fall down dead. But after they had waited a long time and had seen nothing unusual happen to him, they changed their minds and began to say that he was a god.'

The 'native' Maltese are referred to in the Greek text as *'barbaros'* ('barbarians') - an onomatopoeic term simply meaning anyone who couldn't speak Greek. The cold winter rains had begun and so the crew was grateful for the assistance given by the local populace in kindling a fire on the beach. Paul's spontaneous assistance with wood collection led to an 'echidna' *('a viper')* biting his hand. The local people, recognizing the poisonous nature of the snake, waited for a physical reaction, and failing to get one, made the leap from identifying a 'murderer' to a 'god'. They thereby showed a spiritual awareness. albeit in a particularly Gentile manner, similar to that made by the Lystrans in chapter 14.

28:7-10 'Now in the neighbourhood of that place were lands belonging to the leading man of the island, named Publius, who welcomed us and entertained us courteously three days. And it happened that the father of Publius was lying in bed afflicted with recurrent fever and dysentery; and Paul went in to see him and after he had prayed, he laid his hands on him and healed him. After this had happened, the rest of the people on the island who had diseases were coming to him and getting cured. They also honoured us with many marks of respect; and when we were setting sail; they supplied us with all we needed.'

Malta had originally been a wealthy Phoenician colony, and was ruled by Tunisian Carthage from 402 BC until Rome took over in 242 BC.

'Leading man' of the island is 'prôtos', meaning 'chief', a term indicating a Roman-appointed governor. Paul's intervention would therefore be especially appreciated by Luke's Roman addressee, Theophilus, just as it was at the time by the local population of Malta. Having been God's particular recipient of divine care Paul seamlessly moves into being the channel of administering divine care himself by exercising the gift of physical healing, to the great delight of the Maltese people.

'Marks of respect' is ('*timê*'), meaning 'honour' and also 'precious value', descriptive of the many practical expressions of gratitude that overflowed into their generous provisioning of the group's next ship, another Egyptian grain vessel.

28:11-15 'At the end of three months we set sail on an Alexandrian ship which had wintered at the island, and which had the Twin Brothers for its figurehead. After we put in at Syracuse, we stayed there for three days. From there we sailed around and arrived at Rhegium, and a day later a south wind sprang up, and on the second day we came to Puteoli. There we found some brethren, and were invited to stay with them for seven days; and thus we came to Rome. And the brethren, when they heard about us, came from there as far as the Market of Appius and Three Inns to meet us; and when Paul saw them, he thanked God and took courage.'

After three months, Paul and the ship's company managed to get passages for Italy on another Alexandrian corn ship which had itself wintered in Malta. The ship's prow had figure-heads of Castor and Pollux. These two semi-deities were reputed to be the twin sons of Jupiter and Leda, and were believed to watch over sailors. After death, the brothers they were thought to have been taken into heaven, and made stellar constellations under Gemini as the 'Twin Brothers'.

Rhegium (now Reggio) is in Naples, on the coast near the south-west extremity of Italy opposite to Messina, Sicily. Puteoli, on the bay of Naples, is the port of the city of Rome, where the huge navy of the Roman Empire was anchored.

Paul was favoured sufficiently to be granted permission to remain there with fellow believers, while word of their arrival was sent to Rome, some 140 miles distant down the Appian Way. The Roman believers who responded to

Paul's arrival came in two groups, one from the Appian Forum (a travellers' resting place) forty three miles away and the second from The Three Taverns. This was located ten miles nearer Rome and was another well known place of refreshment for travellers.

The presence of these believing strangers, unknown personally to Paul, served to greatly encourage him, strengthening him in his resolve to follow Messiah's leading wherever that might take him.

28:16 'When we entered Rome, Paul was allowed to stay by himself, with the soldier who was guarding him.'

Paul's status, both as a naturally born Roman citizen and as a member of a wealthy Cilician family with particularly elevated standing scholastically and diplomatically, carried with it certain social privileges. One such privilege was to be afforded the comparative luxury of house arrest, rather than needing to endure the privations of the common prison.

We later learn (verse 30) that the expense of this large privately rented house and personal guard was for two years, and that the house was large enough to accommodate all of the leading religious Jews whom Paul invited to come and meet with him there, in addition to the local believers that he also met with.

That these privileges were granted him by no less a personage than the Captain of the Praetorian Guard is extremely significant - Paul was evidently no ordinary prisoner.

'The Captain of the Guard' (Greek: *'stratopedarches'*) literally reads the 'Prætorian Prefect', who, as commander of the Prætorian guard was the highest military authority in the whole city of Rome. The guard acted as personal bodyguards to the Emperor and were an important source of intelligence gathering for him.

Usually there were two such very senior officers, but from A.D. 51 to 62 just one distinguished general, Burrus Aframus, whom Tacitus records ('Annals' 12, 42, 1) had previously been the Emperor Nero's personal tutor, served as the Imperial capital's sole Commander.

As Luke speaks of **'the** captain', this dates Paul's arrival at Rome to be not later than 62AD.

As Paul's personal guard detail would regularly be rotated, so it was that the Gospel message was systematically sown into many Roman military lives. As attested to in Philippians 1:13, the ongoing fruit of this was later widely attested to historically, in later accounts of martyrdom among the Roman army.

28:17-22 'After three days Paul called together those who were the leading men of the Jews, and when they came together, he began saying to them, "Brethren, though I had done nothing against our people or the customs of our fathers, yet I was delivered as a prisoner from Jerusalem into the hands of the Romans. And when they had examined me, they were willing to release me because there was no ground for putting me to death. But when the Jews objected, I was forced to appeal to Caesar, not that I had any accusation against my nation. For this reason, therefore, I requested to see you and to speak with you, for I am wearing this chain for the sake of the hope of Israel. They said to him, We have neither received letters from Judea concerning you, nor have any of the brethren come here and reported or spoken anything bad about you. But we desire to hear from you what your views are; for concerning this sect, it is known to us that it is spoken against everywhere.'"

Jews had been expelled from Rome under Claudius but had returned under Nero. Paul's reputation as a Pharisee and as a product of Gamaliel's school ensured that these most senior fellow Roman Jews would be eager to meet with him. They had yet to receive word of his disputes with the Sanhedrin, but were aware of the new messianic faith expression which they refer to as a sect (of Judaism).

The Greek term here is 'hairesis', meaning 'a choice and an opinion'. The Jews say that it is 'antilegô', meaning 'contradicted' or 'opposed' by fellow religious Jews. Judaism at that time had four major branches, so the arrival of a fifth (Messianic) branch did not unduly trouble the Jews of Rome.

They were therefore keen to hear what Paul had to say about it, and to learn a little more, and Paul was happy to oblige them.

28:23-24 'When they had set a day for Paul, they came to him at his lodging in large numbers; and he was explaining to them by solemnly testifying about the kingdom of God and trying to persuade them concerning Jesus, from both the Law of Moses and from the Prophets, from morning until evening. Some were being persuaded by the things spoken, but others would not believe.'

Paul's rented house was evidently sufficiently commodious to allow the large number of senior Jews in Rome to attend when Paul shared some relevant Hebrew Scriptures with them.

True to form, his audience divided between faith-responders and those still suffering from the spiritual blindness and deafness that Jesus (Matthew 13:14-15) had diagnosed the religious Judeans as suffering from. Jesus had cited Isaiah 6:9-10, and it is this passage that Paul preaches from.

28:25-29 'And when they did not agree with one another, they began leaving after Paul had spoken one parting word, "The Holy Spirit rightly spoke through Isaiah the prophet to your fathers, saying, 'Go to this people and say, You will keep on hearing but not understand; and you will keep on seeing, but will not perceive, for the heart of this people has become dull, and with their ears they can scarcely hear, and they have closed their eyes, otherwise they might see with their eyes, otherwise they might see with their eyes, and hear with their eyes, and hear with their ears, and understand with their heart and return, and return, and I would heal them.'

Isaiah was describing a condition of spiritual obesity, where much knowledge about God has been absorbed, but little done with it, in terms of any practical good towards others.

The common result is a 'waxing gross' (Matthew 13:15), meaning very severe obesity, where the body lays down fat everywhere possible, including the ear lobes and the orbital ridges. In extreme cases the eyes and ears are literally closed with surplus fat, causing actual blindness and deafness. Such an extreme condition was what Jesus had diagnosed the Pharisees as suffering from spiritually.

Jesus had taught that such spiritual obesity was actually preventing the very religious Judean Jews from responding to God as their only hope of spiritual healing.

28:28-29 'Therefore let it be known to you that this salvation of God has been sent to the Gentiles; they will also listen. When he had spoken these words, the Jews departed, having a great dispute among themselves.'

Disputes over religious matters have always been commonplace among Jews, of whom it has been rightly said, 'Two Jews - three opinions!'

Paul had been in this situation many previous occasions, and responded by pointing to the Gentiles as the new recipients of God's grace through Messiah's coming.

28:30-31 'And he stayed two full years in his own rented quarters and was welcoming all who came to him, preaching the kingdom of God and teaching concerning the Lord Jesus Christ with all openness, unhindered.'

Luke's final point, which he leaves in Theophilus' mind and that of the whole Roman judicial system, is that Paul, a fine upstanding Jewish example of Imperial citizenship, was left 'unhindered'. This is *'akôlutôs '*, meaning 'without being restrained'.

Paul's entire life was dedicated to exercising God's word in an 'unrestrained' way.

As he would many years later write to Timothy (following his second arrest), God's word was not chained (2 Timothy 2:9).

It could never be.

Further titles from Templehouse Publishing:

'The New Testament On Women - What Every Man Should Know. ISBN 9780956479815

'The Jesus Discovery – Another Look At Christ's Missing Years' - Joseph the Temple 'Tekton' and Jesus the 'Didaskalos'. ISBN 9780956479808

'El Descubrimiento de Jesus, Otra Mirada a los Anos Perdidos de Cristo' (The Spanish edition of 'The Jesus Discovery.') ISBN9780956479846

'According To Matthew' - A Commentary on the Gospel Of Matthew. ISBN 9780956479839

'Dylan, Depression and Faith' - a Scripture-based analysis of Bob Dylan's lyrics to the present day. ISBN 9780956479822

'The Letter to The Hebrews' - A Commentary On The Book Of Hebrews. ISBN 9780956479853

'Adam, Saint Or Sinner' - Adam as a 'type' of Christ (Romans 5:14). ISBN 9780956479860

'The Medical Gospel Of Luke, As Told To Him By Mary The Mother Of Jesus' ISBN 9780956479877

'Joseph in John, Judas and Jewish Jokes', a commentary on John's Gospel. ISBN 97813265505455

'Runaway Jew - The Truth About Jonah.' ISBN 9781913495077

All these titles are available with a money-back guarantee when purchased directly from the publisher via Templehouse-publishing.com.

They are available in print and digital format.

Other video and audio media formats are available free of charge on YouTube (search for 'Jesus tekton').

www.ingramcontent.com/pod-product-compliance
Lightning Source LLC
Chambersburg PA
CBHW070727160426
43192CB00009B/1342